THE HUMAN FACTOR IN CHANGE

Ron Alan Zimbalist

ScarecrowEducation
Lanham, Maryland • Toronto • Oxford
2005

Published in the United States of America
by ScarecrowEducation
An imprint of The Rowman & Littlefield Publishing Group, Inc.
4501 Forbes Boulevard, Suite 200, Lanham, Maryland 20706
www.scarecroweducation.com

PO Box 317
Oxford
OX2 9RU, UK

British Library Cataloguing in Publication Information Available

Library of Congress Cataloging-in-Publication Data

Zimbalist, Ron Alan, 1944–
  The human factor in change / Ron Alan Zimbalist.
    p. cm.
  Includes bibliographical references and index.
  ISBN 1-57886-216-7 (pbk. : alk. paper)
  1. Organizational change. 2. Organizational change—Psychological aspects.
  I. Title.

  HD58.8.Z55 2005
  658.4'06—dc22

                                        2004026415

♾™ The paper used in this publication meets the minimum requirements of
American National Standard for Information Sciences—Permanence of Paper
for Printed Library Materials, ANSI/NISO Z39.48-1992.
Manufactured in the United States of America.

CONTENTS

FOREWORD

The Essence of the Human Factor: Inside the Arena

Perhaps it was the anticipation of competition or the anxiety of the unknown that forced my adrenaline to surge. "Keep it under control," I said to myself as each step brought me closer to the moment I had trained for. I had always been fascinated with stories from the arena, about individuals who overcame obstacles in their quest for victory. But this was real. It was my time. Like gladiators stepping into the arena for their moment of truth, I was filled with a feeling of uncertainty that froze time without a thought of the future. I was about to step into the arena, where all eyes would focus on my words and actions. Others had tried and failed, and I wondered if I would be the next victim. As I stepped into the library for that first staff meeting I saw a staff that had struggled through eight years of pain and disappointment.

The following six years saw a new vision shape a high-performing team that would culminate with successful grants and awards for the once-troubled school. Ego was checked at the door as the staff worked together for a common cause that would lead to a remarkable turnaround.

It's tough in the arena. Educators in America face challenges that not only test their resolve but the very nature of their beliefs. What happens to those bright-eyed, enthusiastic teachers who start their careers determined to change the world? Whether they realize it or not, they *are* changing the world, one child at a time. Like the ticking of a clock, change never stops.

Because life is a succession of changes, the only way we can fully enjoy it is to adapt to those changes. The pursuit of change is actually a personal journey toward an improved condition. I believe the human factor is the most powerful ingredient in any form of social interaction. The human factor is just that—it's all things human. It's about people. It's about understanding, accepting, working with, motivating, and respecting people in any social environment.

The present moment is always subject to unsuspecting challenges. The past is all we really have; the present is but a blink of an eye, and the future hasn't happened yet. So how do school administrators keep the faith when consumed with the battle inside the arena? What do we say to overworked teachers who are pushed to the brink of a career change?

Of all the tasks school administrators face, perhaps the greatest is developing quality teachers. What do we say to teachers who are disillusioned or complacent, to those are still enthusiastic and dedicated, or to those who are skeptical because of unfulfilled dreams? We tell them that the destination is worth the journey.

Perhaps the essence of the human factor can be illustrated in my final address to a staff that had overcome the challenges of years of disappointment and unfulfilled expectations. The school's negative reputation had changed to celebrations of success leading to a remarkable turnaround.

While traveling along the path of your career, someday you will remember that we did something special here. Together, we not only overcame the pressures inherent in education but also thrived in an arena where others are casting judgment on public education. I'm reminded of the pressures associated with deadlines, grants, committees, grades, parents, and students. We have raised academic standards, improved technology, implemented innovation, and inspired students to take personal responsibility for their actions. Education today is an exhilarating challenge.

Through the years, I have been most proud of the fact that you have kept the faith in the art of education by putting kids first. You have touched the lives of young people in ways that may not be evident for years. Regardless of the obstacles you faced, you made an effort to improve the lives of those who will follow. Who knows the impact you have had on a youngster's personality? Perhaps they will remember your smile or the patience you showed when they needed you when you were in a hurry but you stopped anyway. Maybe it was the way you took the time to explain things in a way they understood or always made them feel good just being around you.

They'll forget the lesson, the tests, and the final scores, but they will remember you.

Could it be that in you, their teacher, they saw order, caring, and the love they wish they had at home? For most of your students, you'll never know the mark you've made on their lives. That's the way it is for teachers.

You try your best, you stand for what you believe in, you continue to grow professionally; and just maybe in years to come, someone will stop by and say, "I remember when you were my teacher. You made a difference for me. Thanks!"

I

THE SPIRIT OF CHANGE

1

DREAMS

You see things; and you say "Why?" but I dream things that never were; and I say "Why not?"

—George Bernard Shaw

What does it take to turn around an organization? It seems Americans have always been fascinated with success stories of underdogs making good. We have seen businesses on the verge of bankruptcy suddenly acquire new dynamic leadership and make dramatic turnarounds. In education, we have heard how troubled schools found the formula for success and made the most of it. Turnaround is about overcoming obstacles. It's rooting for the underdog. It's the story of David and Goliath. It's Rocky going the distance. It's about winning.

In reality, such stories may be few and far between, although current literature does substantiate numerous success stories in both business and education. In *The Human Factor in Change,* we will identify key elements of the change process and some of the best practices that are consistent with successful change efforts. Research indicates that change involves more than one charismatic leader charging up the hill to victory. The change process represents a complex combination of factors that, when assembled in the proper order, can make reform possible.

Actually, winning is a journey rather than a destination. It is found somewhere beyond the land of dreams where harmony reigns. Found between hope and faith, it is concealed by doubt and arrogance; yet it is revealed in simplicity. You may have passed through such a place while traveling along the path of life. There are no directions or maps, because the voyage never ends. It is not a place defined by things but rather a state of unity where the common cause is greater than any pursuit of individual satisfaction.

Sounds rather esoteric, doesn't it? Perhaps, but upon closer examination, the essence of the human factor is revealed. What *is* the human factor, you ask? Through the following pages we will explore the most powerful ingredient found in any form of social interaction. The human factor is just that, it's all things human. It's about people. It's about understanding, accepting, cooperating, motivating, and respecting people in any social environment. Whether your career is at the administrative, management, or labor level, you will experience social interaction and eventually adapt to change. Actually, the human factor is obvious. It's about treating people right and gaining their confidence. Yet if it is so obvious, why are so many organizations struggling to find meaningful improvement?

The thread of change weaves through history without respect to culture or geographic region. The pursuit of change is actually a journey toward an improved personal condition. It doesn't matter whether you worship the god of profit or face the challenges of an altruistic calling; the human journey for fulfillment is based upon change.

So where is this place where harmony reigns, and how do we get there? We start our journey by exploring this nation's quest for personal improvement.

What is it that drives people to acquire more than they have? Is life merely a game governed by the rules of self-gratification? A new century finds our affluent society indoctrinated in the philosophy of acquisition. If it feels good, it must be good. If two ounces are adequate, ten ounces must be better. Is it true that whoever dies with the most toys wins? For this fantasy culture, perception is fast becoming greater than reality.

Now more than ever, we live in a time where dreams tend to morph into facts. Often the depths of our dreams determine the passion of our commitments. If we choose to follow a dream, we choose to accept change—because whether we like it or not, change is an inescapable fact of life. Whether globally, nationally, or personally, we live in a time where change dominates the human experience. Never has there been such a vast array of resources available to implement change as today. A close examination of the change process reveals that some individuals and organizations have learned how to use the phenomenon of change to bring about positive results while others still struggle in the mire of the status quo. You can hide from it, run from it, even ignore it, but just as sure as the rivers flow and winds blow, change will happen. Therefore, the question we all face is: How can we influence change to bring about desired results?

Many people never experience the exhilaration of being part of a smoothly functioning team. All too often, career conversations center around dissatisfaction and finger pointing rather than the fulfillment associated with winning. It is obvious when walking into a staff lunchroom. Does the conversation suddenly stop or turn to whispers when administrators enter the room? At that moment, the line is drawn, the troops align themselves into a mode of dissatisfaction. Such behavior may take place subconsciously and spontaneously or be deeply ingrained into the existing culture of the organization. An alert leader keeps a finger on the pulse of the organization and seizes opportunities to bridge the gap of mistrust. *The Human Factor* is about building and healing on a twenty-four/seven schedule.

So check your ego at the door as we examine how successful leaders use the change process to their advantage. We will discover that the ability to implement change is actually inherent in all of us. It is when we understand the nature of individuals within the context of their organizations that we are able to apply the elements of change successfully. Successful leaders learn how to skillfully tap into the inherent nature of change in order to bring about desired results.

If we believe in the American Dream, we must also believe that a personal state of satisfaction is unacceptable. Historically, Americans have been a restless people. Not satisfied with what is known, we reach out for the unknown. Americans are also an ingenious people, continually nurturing the germination of innovation. Perhaps the ability to dream for a better life lies beyond a mere physical state of contentment. In the United States, change has become synonymous with a quest for a brighter future. That desire for personal improvement is the essence of the American Spirit. Our ancestors had it. Just think of those hardy souls who dared to leave the security of England to cross the rugged Atlantic in their small boats, only to discover an inhospitable land of swamps, harsh climate, and hostile Algonquian natives. What were they thinking of, to take on such a dangerous adventure?

The names of their three ships reveal the depth of their life-or-death commitment for change—*Susan Constant, Godspeed,* and *Discovery*. Eventually naming their first settlement Jamestown, in honor of King James I, on May 24, 1607, our first pioneers were actually merchants sent out by the London Company of England. That's right—that great expedition was initially a business venture as well as a desire to spread the word of God to the far reaches of the earth.

What would it be like to take a stand for a personal belief knowing the decision could cost your life? I've often wondered if I could bet my life on my commitment. In Philadelphia on July 4, 1776, fifty-six men knew full well they would be marked for treason once they signed a document titled the Declaration of Independence. Every American wearing our country's military uniform is ready to lay it on the line for what they believe. Can members of the private or public sectors do any less than give their all to make life better for others? The list of extraordinary exploits by those who dared to sacrifice what was known in search for the unknown has become the backbone of the American Spirit.

The odds were against our ancestors who dared to seek change. It would be safe to assume that those adventurers from the past were told that their plans for a new life just wouldn't work. Have you ever had what you thought was a bright new idea only to have someone put it down, by throwing a bucket of stagnation on it? *Been there and done that. It won't work here.*

When we view events in time, it is easy to assume the position of a Monday-morning quarterback. Those who made history did so without the benefit of instant replay. I have often wondered if the courage of the past still exists in this affluent society. When I refer to the affluent society in America, I use the term in general comparison to the rest of the world. According to the U.S. Census Bureau and the Department of Health and Human Services, the level of poverty of a family of four with two children is $17,463. Such an income in many third-world countries would be viewed as wealth, not poverty. *Serving the World's Poor, Profitably,* by C. K. Prahlad and Allan Hammond (2002), published by the Harvard Business School, found that 65 percent of the world's population earns less than $2,000 per year (p. 2). In other words, over four billion people are $15,000 below the U.S. poverty level. The issues of world poverty are as complex as the existing barriers that keep people trapped in their present conditions. But regardless of one's position or station in life, there are always dreams.

In recent years, I have wondered how our nation would respond to extraordinary circumstances. Have we become so complacent in our affluent lifestyles that we are content to avoid commitments that reach beyond our immediate comfort zones? Or is the quest for change actually imbedded in the American Spirit? Of the many examples of ordinary people accomplishing extraordinary undertakings, a few events stand out in recent history. The American Spirit has proved to be alive and well, as evidenced by our nation's response to monumental events on a global scale. On December 7, 1941, America began an undertaking so remarkable that the results couldn't have been scripted in Hollywood. The nation stood together, utilizing its physical and personal resources to rise up and defeat a foreign threat to the American way of life.

Seldom has a single event made an impact on all humanity as one did on July 16, 1945. It was just another hot July morning in the dry New Mexico desert when life changed for all of us. Code-named "The Gadget," the world changed forever at 5:29 AM, when six years of research culminated in the explosion of the first atomic bomb. Three weeks later the world changed again when 260,000 Japanese were killed at Hiroshima by a single atomic bomb. Even now we live under the shadow of that mushroom cloud.

The world changed yet again on October 4, 1957, when the Soviet Union launched Sputnik I, the first man-made satellite to orbit the earth. Uneasiness gripped the United States as our adversary of the cold war had reached into space. At that time my father was an electronic technician; as a boy I listened on short-wave radio to the beeps and blips coming from that space probe. The trajectory was publicized in the *Los Angeles Times*, and I joined my space-geek friends on a cold fall evening to watch the satellite silently pass over southern California. For us, science fiction had come to life. This was better than the Blob or *The Day the Earth Stood Still.* Were the Russians spying on us, or was Sputnik really a nuclear weapon hanging over our heads? Once again we learned that change brings uncertainty. In the following year, the United States repeatedly tried, but failed, to match the Soviet's success in space. American ingenuity and resolve eventually met the challenge, not only entering the space race but claiming victory when an American took that "one small step for mankind," setting foot on the moon just twelve years later. The far-reaching effects of the space race changed our lives as new products and government agencies were created out of necessity and competition. Beyond the obvious technological advances that were thrust upon our already-complicated lifestyles, a new anxiety about survival fueled speculation that now we were really living in the end times.

My family lived in Shadow Hills, in the rural foothills east of the San Fernando Valley, where nothing ever happened. One day a couple of large trucks stopped at the corner of Sunland Boulevard and Wheatland, and a crew of men began scurrying around erecting something that looked at first like a new telephone pole. I lived on a hillside that overlooked the valley and could see the construction about two hundred yards away. It didn't look like a telephone pole after a while; there was something else going on there, and within minutes I was on the phone to my fifth-grade partners Doug and Wayne. This was news, and as members of the Sunland Astronomical Society (actually, we were the only members), we had to check out this mysterious activity.

When the dust cleared and the trucks drove away, a thick pole had been installed on the corner. It was not like any telephone pole we had ever seen. Atop the pole was a large cylinder with louvers cut into the sides. Over the next few weeks we learned the purpose of that mysterious pole. In school, our principal held an assembly and explained the importance of the new safety drills we would soon be practicing. Fire drills, "drop and cover," and evacuation drills would become a part of our education. At 10:00 a.m. on the first Monday of the month, air raid sirens would sound throughout the area, and we would practice our new drills in preparation for the ultimate disaster. Wow, the space race and the threat of nuclear attack had come to Shadow Hills.

Does it take a crisis to bring out the best in America? Could it be that the spirit is alive in ordinary people who actually accomplish extraordinary feats every day? On September 11, 2001, I saw our country renew its attitude about patriotism and come together as I had never seen in my lifetime. As a young man my reference point of patriotism had been the divided image of Vietnam and the skepticism that struggle produced. But after 9/11 pride was back. The spirit was evident everywhere. It was suddenly cool to display an American flag. The spirit of America was still alive, and I believe our American ancestors would have been proud of how our country came together in a time of need.

Now, as in the past, acts of courage and determination require faith that something better is in store. That spirit of adventure was eloquently described by Theodore Roosevelt: "No man is worth his salt who is not ready at all times to risk his body, to risk his well-being, to risk his life, in a great cause" (Brownlow 1997, 4). The chapters of our country's history are filled with countless true stories of those who were not afraid to climb the mountains of danger or cross the valleys of sorrow in their personal quest for a better life. As we look deeper into the decisions those hearty pioneers must have faced, it becomes clear that our lives today would not be what they are if those before us had not been willing to change their own lives.

It has been said that Americans are a bottom-line people. We want to know the best price, the end result, the final score, and ultimately, who won. Whether we like it or not, our society is driven by competition. A national fascination with the Lombardian philosophy—winning isn't everything, it's the only thing—has moved from the football fields to corporate boardrooms and even small offices across America. So often that great coach's message has been misinterpreted. What he actually said was, "Winning is not everything, but making the effort to win is" (VinceLombardi.com). Vince Lombardi will always be remembered for that misquoted statement; yet how many of us remember another statement he made about personal determination? "The spirit, the will to win and the will to excel, these are the things that endure and these are the qualities that are so much more important than any of the events that occasion them" (VinceLombardi.com).

A closer look at competition reveals a fine line between winning and losing. Use your imagination, and let's travel to the prestigious Masters Golf Tournament at the Augusta National golf course, where a swelling gallery of fans anticipates the final putt on the eighteenth green. They hold their breath as the small white ball rolls toward the cup only to stop one-eighth of an inch from victory.

Look at the modern Olympic Games, where a variety of incredible human feats are measured in milliseconds and fractions of inches. Every four years, a highlight of the Olympics is the anticipated race of the century to determine the world's fastest human. Time seems to stand still, yet it passes like a blur after the gun sounds. Magnificent athletes exert every muscle in their highly trained bodies, sprinting toward the hundred-meter finish line. An electronic beam signals the winner less than an inch ahead of the competition.

Now, visualize an enormous circular parking area surrounding a magnificent arena. Nighttime lights twinkle, reflected in the rain-soaked pavement. Inside the arena, seventeen thousand screaming fans watch the final seconds disappear on the game clock as forty-eight minutes of competition in the National Basketball Association comes to an end, only one point making the difference between success and failure.

Or does it? Could it be that winning or losing is actually just perception? Oh, I know what you're thinking. Winning is really all that matters, and any attempt to rationalize otherwise is a cop-out. After all, winning is the American way. It's John Wayne, the New York Yankees, and Bill Gates. In business, you either get the account or you don't. Achievement is the end result and ultimately becomes the factor upon which you will be evaluated. Is a person of less value when attempting change, only to come up short of the desired goal?

Is the journey greater than the destination? An ancient Chinese proverb reminds us, "A journey of a thousand miles must begin with a single step." We have seen how the phenomenon of change alters lives and shapes history. But as the Chinese proverb reminds us, change must have a beginning before there can be an end. If we are to take control of personal change, the proverb tells us, it is important to take initial action toward a desired destination. But which way do we turn in order to take that first step? Visualizing the destination provides direction. It's that vision thing. It is best to know where we are going before we take the first step. Much has been said about the leadership provided by President John F. Kennedy when he challenged the nation before a joint session of Congress on May 25, 1961.

> I believe that this nation should commit itself to achieving the goal, before this decade is out of landing a man on the moon and returning him safely to the earth. Finally, our greatest asset in this struggle is the American people—their willingness to pay the price for these programs—to understand and accept a long struggle. (National Archives and Records Administration 2003, John F. Kennedy)

If the purpose of examining history is to find guides for the future, it would serve us well to heed such wisdom from the past. As far back as 1713, the English essayist Joseph Addison spoke of an inner desire shared by all cultures: "A day, an hour of virtuous liberty is worth a whole eternity in bondage" (Bartlett 2002). The records of antiquity are full of examples of human subjugation, but even in the darkest conditions of human bondage, the spark of courageous acts of independence eventually grew into flames of freedom. Sometimes courage is displayed when least expected. Whether from the trials of a prisoner of war, such as Senator John McCain of Arizona, or the unyielding efforts of simple people working their fingers to the bone in substandard housing just to keep their families together rather than be trapped in a maze of welfare, the inner drive for an improved life can move mountains.

Over two hundred years ago, the architects of our democracy understood that liberty required change. It was Thomas Jefferson who clearly established the blueprint for individual liberty: "We hold these truths to be self-evident, that all men are created equal; that they are endowed by their Creator with certain inalienable rights; that among these are life, liberty and the pursuit of happiness" (National Archives and Records Administration 2003, Thomas Jefferson). Our nation's desire to pursue something beyond our current condition has actually become the essence of the American experience.

In 1963, Martin Luther King Jr., shared his dream with a country that had long tolerated inequality: "I have a dream that one day on the red hills of Georgia the sons of former slaves and the sons of former slave-owners will be able to sit down together at the table of brotherhood" (members.aol.com/klove01/martinsp.htm). It was then that a nation saw one man's dream become a rallying cry for millions, who came to share the same dream.

So it is that the term "American Dream" generally refers to an improved personal lifestyle with the freedom to achieve one's potential. Each American views the Dream from a personal perspective. It may result in a journey over time or just a brief adaptation of a habit. Realizing how hard it is to change a habit, most people would be happy with a little change. Change is easier said than done. Think of those who are seeking a way to lose weight or to kick the nicotine habit. The business world recognizes the potential for marketing the change process. From self-help to weight loss, billions of dollars are spent every year on efforts to initiate personal change.

Regardless of one's dream, achievement requires action, risk, and eventually, change. As we look at the historical forces that have put the United States into its current position on the world stage, we find an insatiable quest for growth. Some would argue that the effects of such an appetite become all consuming, eventually devouring everything in its path. Our history of expansion and affluence has been looked down upon by skeptics and by cultures that tend to view our world position with envy or hatred. The events of September 11, 2001, demonstrate how perverted philosophies from mainstream cultures can manifest themselves into destructive actions. It should also be remembered that Americans are a compassionate people, not only rooted in independence but also altruistically dedicated to helping people in need. The dual nature of America's effort in Afghanistan during operation Enduring Freedom, begun in 2001, illustrates the dichotomy of our country's parallel philosophy. America not only vigorously attacked terrorists in Afghanistan but at the same time delivered and distributed food and medical supplies to the vast majority of the Afghan people.

Regardless of one's personal interpretation of history, it is clear that growth, whether personal, collective, or nationalistic, can develop only as a result of change. The elements of change are evident in all cultures. From birth to death, change is an inescapable fact of life itself. To some, change is a magical ingredient that transforms people and organizations. We will see that not all change is desirable and that careful planning through skilled leadership can not only improve human performance but improve life and relationships as well. When you think about it, change transcends culture. It seems logical to assume that regardless of one's physical location or position in life, the spirit of personal improvement shapes one's destiny. In the American culture, who doesn't want to improve his or her position in life? Who doesn't want something better for their children? To dream is to visualize something different than what exists.

In his Day of Affirmation address at the University of Capetown in South Africa on June 6, 1966, Robert Kennedy spoke of dreams and of overcoming the dangers of complacency.

> First, is the danger of futility: the belief there is nothing one man or one woman can do against the enormous array of the world's ills—against misery and ignorance, injustice and violence. Yet many of the world's greatest movements, of thought and action, have flowed from the work of a single man. A young monk began the Protestant Reformation, a young general extended an empire from Macedonia to the borders of the earth, and a young woman reclaimed the territory of France. It was a young Italian explorer who discovered the New World, and thirty-two-year-old Thomas Jefferson proclaimed that all men are created equal. (National Archives and Records Administration 2003, Robert Kennedy)

If dreams are the stuff that accomplishments are made of, change must be the process that turns dreams into reality. When faced with challenges great and small, inaction can be summarized by a phrase given to me years ago by Elena Rodriguez, a fifth-grade teacher in East Los Angeles: If you always do what you always did, you will always get what you always got.

Through the years, researchers have investigated at great length the elements of successful individuals and organizations. The results of such detailed analyses have led to countless books, conferences, and popular how-to gurus who have been revered by success seekers everywhere. In spite of this national trend of emulation, the proof of true leadership is found in results over time. History records the efforts of visionary leaders who have made their marks on countries and organizations. Those who are successful are in it for the long haul; they are committed. Leaders who inspire must also take ownership and nurture their vision until it becomes reality. Change is not easy. That is precisely why President Kennedy followed up his challenge of putting a man on the moon when he spoke at Rice University in Houston, Texas, on September 12, 1962.

> We choose to go to the moon. We choose to go to the moon in this decade and do the other things, not because they are easy, but because they are hard, because that goal will serve to organize and measure the best of our energies and skills, because that challenge is one that we are willing to accept, one we are unwilling to postpone, and one which we intend to win, and the others too. (National Archives and Records Administration 2003, John F. Kennedy)

We have seen how dreams have filled the hearts of those who wanted change. If we are to move mountains, change must become reality. Whether leading an organization, coaching a team, or building a relationship, we will find there is no room for doubt and arrogance. When individuals work together for a common cause, harmony reigns. If harmony means some sort of euphoric equilibrium, we must remember that most people will never reach such a state in their workplaces. For employees who will never experience that place where harmony reigns, the best that can be expected is a few years of mutual respect while accomplishing something worthwhile. They will read with envy about others who reached the pinnacle of human performance and wonder how they did it.

Could it be that the dark side of the human factor is the greatest enemy of positive change? Doubt and arrogance are powerful forces. Is that why some organizations fail to grow? It can be safely said that when there is harmony among people, self-serving interests are replaced with commitments for the common good.

T. E. Lawrence, better known as Lawrence of Arabia, was considered a dreamer in his day. That is not a bad thing, since the future starts with dreams. Lawrence wrote of dreams and reality: "All men dream, but unequally. Those that dream at night in the dusty recesses of their minds awaken the next day to find that their dreams were just vanity. But those who dream during the day with their eyes wide open are dangerous men; they act out their dreams to make them reality" (Goodman 1997).

Good things start with dreams.

2

BE CAREFUL WHAT
YOU WISH FOR

They shouldn't have done it that way! If I could, I would . . . !

We all have opinions about the decisions made at the management level of our organizations. The press criticizes politicians, laborers cast doubt on managers, and followers question leaders. It is natural to have opinions and believe we have better solutions. In spite of all of our opinions, doesn't it seem that most organizations continue to follow established patterns and avoid significant change unless absolutely necessary? Is anyone even listening to our suggestions? Maybe we are too reluctant to stand up and voice our opinions in a constructive way. If management continues to make decisions that we feel are wrong for our organizations, will we succumb to the temptations of becoming a silent critic, a sniper, or worst of all, a chronic negative employee?

But what if the opportunity came your way? What if you could do it right?

Does life really work like that?

Sometimes it does. When the right situation comes along, seize the opportunity to test your theories and build a better mousetrap. That opportunity came for me, and it was to draw on the skills I had learned from a career as a teacher, coach, business owner, and school administrator. How would you like to open a new school? If I had the chance, it wouldn't be just another school. It would be a model of efficient learning, in a new state-of-the-art facility. Ah, the smell of fresh paint, new furniture, and heating and lighting systems that actually worked.

Coming off a successful school turnaround effort that had culminated with Distinguished School awards, I was ready for a new challenge. After all, the grass is always greener on the other side of the fence, isn't it? I had visions of Camelot high on a hill, with sparkling fixtures, smiling teachers, and perfect children. This was going to be great.

It was a cool Saturday morning in November when the superintendent invited me for a tour of the district's new schools. I had been selected to open the new middle school, and now it was decision time. He seemed to be an honest and caring man, but I could see he was a shrewd leader who definitely had a plan for this tour.

We drove to the high school first. It was a beautifully designed glass and steel structure spreading over sixty acres of manicured lawns. The middle school and elementary schools were all new, clean, and free from graffiti. My anticipation grew; it was obvious that he was saving the new site for the end of our tour. I tried to be cool and not display my eagerness. We drove from the city into the country along a two-lane road with irrigation ditches on each side. There was nothing but open fields for miles around, just a few old buildings about a mile down the road. I wondered where the new school site was going to be. Finally he turned into the parking lot in front of those old buildings. I thought he was just using the lot to turn around. "Well, here we are," he said.

Where was Camelot? It was not even on a hill. Suddenly the sparkle vanished from my vision as I focused on the drab modular rooms, painted an ugly dark brown and rust color. The old school had a decent-looking multipurpose room; the rest was depressing. He said the site was currently used by the district's alternative school and that it would soon move into a new facility. Excuse me—but this looked like a medium-security detention facility. I suddenly had a feeling of relief, remembering I hadn't committed to this position yet and was still a finalist for a small-school superintendent position in another district.

In his patient yet optimistic way, the superintendent described his vision for this site. The district was negotiating to purchase the adjacent ten acres and would build a new gym, administrative offices, classrooms, a library, and science labs. The old buildings would be renovated inside and out before school opened in seven months. The new construction would be completed in about a year. He described the tremendous growth in the area; within a short time new homes, shopping centers, and parks would encircle this school. "This project will be a great opportunity for the right person to design programs and have input on a new facility," he said in his most convincing manner.

I don't think so, I thought to myself.

Over the next two weeks I wrestled with the decision of whether to stay put, take the leadership of a small district, or open the new school. When faced with challenges both great and small we naturally tap into our personal bank account of emotions, and it doesn't hurt to seek wise council along the way. Our decisions ultimately affect our families and careers as we seek to do the right thing. The excitement of opening a new school was still there, even if I would have to live in peasant huts before climbing the hill to Camelot.

Little did I know that the events of the next four years would test my skills and patience beyond any rational expectation. I spent the first seven months in the district office designing programs, meeting with architects, and preparing budgets, while hiring staff. Building a program that would meet the needs of the children in the community was our first priority. The superintendent supported my efforts to bring the whole-child concept of middle school education to the district. The challenge of using available resources to support program needs was creatively met by our young teachers.

Circumstances shaped my original vision of Camelot; it soon became evident that the luster of sparkling new buildings was secondary to the heart and soul of the school. Seventy-five percent of the new staff was hired from outside the district, and most were first- or second-year teachers. We were creating an educational environment rich with talented, enthusiastic teachers who genuinely cared for children. What a concept!

District reading and math scores revealed a strong need for remediation, so we changed direction with curriculum and implemented a direct-instruction model in reading and math. The Connecting Math Concepts curriculum was introduced, along with the SRA reading-intervention program. Technology became a way of doing business rather than an additional burden for untrained teachers. A sizable investment brought a hands-on technology lab and video production studio to the meager campus. In the technology lab, students would work in collaborative teams exploring modules of aerodynamics, rocketry, electricity, lasers, and computer technology. It became common to see teams of two or three students setting up news cameras on campus. Every morning a student-generated TV broadcast brought school news and character-education features to all the networked classrooms in the school. Teachers were working together in teams dedicated to help all students achieve success. The old buildings received a bright coat of paint, and an updated fiber-based network brought the Internet to all rooms. Maybe this would be Camelot after all. We were like a Model T on the outside with a Rolls Royce engine on the inside.

School opened in August with great expectations; we eagerly anticipated breaking ground and moving into the new school the following summer. That's when circumstances turned into a comedy—or should I say, a tragedy. A diary of disaster followed, a sequence of events that would not only test the limits of our patience but drive the forces of creative endurance for all of us.

August 2000: Change of Mind

- The owner of the future school site changes his mind and decides not to sell the ten acres to the west of the existing buildings. He offers to sell the ten acres to the east instead. The district is forced to return to the architect to have plans redesigned for the new location.
- Unable to beat the county deadline for starting new projects, the plan is put on hold until escrow closes. According to a city ordinance, site excavation for construction projects must break ground prior an October deadline or wait until the dry period in the spring.

October 2000: Bad Timing

- The Environmental Protection Agency (EPA) files suit with the county stating that housing development in the area was moving too fast and not considering the consequences to wildlife. It seems our school site is in an area native to the giant garter snake and red-tailed hawk. A federal judge stops all construction in the basin until future development can be reviewed. The district is caught up in the process and can't break ground. Negotiations stall with the owner of the ten acres.
- State budget warnings arise as potential energy shortage looms for that winter.
- The staff celebrates the first new baby born to one of our young teachers.

December 2000: Energy Crisis

- Energy costs skyrocket throughout California as state financial reserves are used to purchase expensive energy. Having bought a house in the area in September, we see our electric and gas bills soar from $120 a month to over $500 by December.
- The state spends billions of dollars from reserves to purchase additional high-cost energy as the governor scrambles for federal assistance.
- Escrow with the land owner finally closes on the new ten-acre site and the district can mobilize their construction plan.

January–February 2001: Budget Cuts

- California's borrowing capacity is reduced as result of the expenditure of all its reserves, and the state legislature prepares for emergency measures to meet the growing financial crisis.
- The state reduces education funding across the board. Categorical programs are cut 20 percent; districts are forced to dip into their own reserves.
- Los Angeles files suit to divert state school construction funds to the high-population areas in the south.
- The district realizes it will not receive the $9 million owed by the state. The board meets to discuss budget cuts. The architect completes the school plans and submits them to the State Architect for approval.

April 2001: Decision Time

- The state announces further budget cuts in education.
- Energy costs throughout the state finally stabilize.
- Forced to use reserves and facing more state education cuts, the district trustees debate the future of the new school. The community packs an emotional April board meeting to support the construction of the new school. By a four-to-one vote the board agrees to build the school in one phase rather than over time. The board faces the challenge of securing funding in a time of financial crisis. Unaffected by the events

surrounding the new school construction, however, both students and staff continue to find the year positive.

May 2001: No More Snakes

- In Washington, D.C., the EPA is satisfied, and the building moratorium in our area is lifted.
- Architectural plans are approved by Department of State Architects (DSA).
- The district identifies funding for the new school through certificate of participation bonds, along with a bond measure to be placed on the ballot in the November election.
- The $12 million school project is opened for construction bids.
- The second baby born to our young staff brings genuine shouts of joy.

June 2001: A New Promise

- School ends on a positive note. Planning continues for the opening of school in August. Projections indicate that enrollment will double, to over six hundred students.
- I prepare to work all summer planning schedules and hiring staff to fill new positions. The capacity of the old facility will be pushed to the limit with new enrollment, but enthusiasm remains high, with a promise that construction will soon begin.

August 2001: A Beehive

- The overcrowded school opens, with some students sitting on floors while additional furniture is borrowed and purchased. Students are, however, excited with new opportunities in technology and at the same time eagerly work with teachers to build a positive school culture.
- A construction contract is awarded.

October 2001: The Earth Shakes

- Amid further shouts of joy from the staff, construction begins. The entire outdoor basketball court area is removed and construction fencing is put in place. The physical education department has to adapt its program to make do without an outdoor area. Activities move into the small multipurpose room, which is also used as the school's cafeteria.

- Quality instruction continues as bulldozers literally shake the walls of adjacent rooms. Students think it's cool. Teacher patience is tested, but the construction noise becomes music to the ears of teachers anxious to see the new school finally started.
- Patience and enthusiasm continues to be challenged under overcrowded conditions.

November 2001: The Buildings Arise

- The steel frame of the new office and student services building is put in place. In an emotional moment only two months after 9/11, workers place an American flag high atop the steel frame.
- Construction continues at a brisk pace as concrete footings are poured for two classroom clusters, the library, a gym, and science buildings.
- Students are kept up to date with the progress of construction by video broadcasts from the contractor.

January 2002: The Mystery

- The once-busy construction site gradually settles into silence. At first no one pays much attention, but it becomes obvious that work crews have dwindled to three men sharing a hammer. Something is wrong.
- A different subcontractor begins work on the new outdoor eating area connecting to the existing multipurpose room. Construction fencing seals off the center of the school, restricting student passage to narrow pathways lined with temporary fencing and bright orange cones.

May 2002: Ghost Town

- Our worst fears are realized when the general contractor files for bankruptcy and is unable to complete the project. Negotiations continue through the summer between the bonding company, the district's legal council, and the contractor.

- An eerie quiet falls over the partially completed buildings as students gaze through chain-link fencing wondering what has happened.

August 2002: Enrollment Swells

- The third year of the new school begins with ever-growing enrollment forcing the district to bring in nine temporary twelve-by-sixteen-foot portables that looked like boxcars.
- No vacation again, as I work all summer developing supervision schedules to accommodate new traffic patterns, new teachers, more students, and more inconvenience. With all rooms filled to capacity, three teachers agree to become itinerant instructors, moving from room to room each period.

October 2002: The Rains Come

- The incomplete buildings resemble a ghost town. Weeds begin to take over the 70-percent-completed construction site. The bankruptcy is still in negotiation.
- As if the construction problems aren't enough, Mother Nature steps in and decides that this will be a year of heavy rains in central California. Rain is a good thing, except when buildings have no windows or doors. It is wet inside and out. By the end of November the windows and doors are boarded up with plywood. Now the site really takes on that depressed, condemned look.

December 2002: Good News and Bad News

- Good news—the bonding company selects another contractor to complete the project. Limited work begins amid renewed shouts of joy from the staff.
- Bad news—because of the heavy rains, mold is discovered in the finished walls of three buildings. Work is stopped. Mold and water deterioration is also found in the unfinished walls of the science and math buildings. Debate begins on the proper method for mold treatment.

February 2003: Adjusting, Again

- Renovation of the multipurpose room and kitchen begins. The kitchen is moved to a partially renovated classroom and becomes only a heat-and-serve facility for pizza, burritos, and chips. From the offices to the makeshift cafeteria, wires and empty conduits hang from ceilings and walls.
- More confusion follows as the contractor tears up the grass fields in way of the new playing fields. Now the physical education program has not only no outdoor area but no grass area and no multipurpose room. Once again creativity is tested through patience. Portable basketball goals are set up along the fire exit road behind the classrooms.

April 2003: Moving Day

- The offices the library and two classroom clusters are finally complete. Teachers move into their new rooms, amid more shouts of joy.
- Work slowly continues on other buildings.

August 2003: Year Four

- The school year begins with 850 students, but the end is finally in sight.
- Construction continues until the gym and science buildings are completed.

December 2003: The End

- Construction fencing is finally removed as the new facility is occupied by teachers and students.
- With no energy left for shouts of joy, the exhausted staff gives a solemn sign of relief.

Call it a comedy of errors or just growing pains, but the vision finally became reality. The process was costly not only financially but emotionally as well. Camelot was not as shiny as I had once thought it would be. We learn from every experience in life, and this venture reaffirmed that quality comes from building positive relationships. Leaders can set the tone, but the strength of the team comes from within. The teachers, the students, and the culture we created formed memories that will outlive all the trials of that construction fiasco. A wonderful facility is nice, but people make the difference between success and failure. Through it all we found that the human factor kept the school together in the face of frustration and discouragement.

When it was over, I was asked if I would do it again. After pausing a few moments, I could only say, "Be careful what you wish for, because you never really know what the future will bring." I wouldn't wish such a difficult project on anyone. Yet real joy came from creating an educational environment that brought people together and motivated students to achieve. We found that overcoming obstacles is not about what you want but rather what you do with what you have. We were able to have quality even when surrounded by chaos.

I believe Walt Disney understood the essence of the human factor. Asked why his magical kingdom was so successful, he said, "You can design and create, and build the most wonderful place in the world. But it takes people to make the dream a reality."

3

FOR BETTER
OR WORSE

There is a certain relief in change, even though it be from bad to worse! As I have often found in traveling in a stagecoach, that it is often a comfort to shift one's position, and be bruised in a new place.

—Washington Irving

In light of our nation's trials and tribulations, wouldn't it have been easier for our ancestors if they had been merely satisfied with their current state of equilibrium and just made the best of their situations in their homelands? Standing still appears easier than stepping forward. If our early settlers had taken the easy way, there would be no American Dream as we know it. The status quo would have ruled, and individual liberty could have turned into something like a Marxist system of social stagnation. Standing still or, what's worse allowing, token change says that we are satisfied with our product. What if our students were satisfied with only partial information? They would find themselves at a disadvantage as they competed for places in the new international job market.

I once knew a young man, a tenth-grader, who was satisfied with what he knew and thought efforts to expand his knowledge were boring. One of his history essays reflected his satisfaction with academic status quo:

The nineteenth century was a time of a great many thoughts and inventions. People stopped reproducing by hand and started reproducing by machine.

Soon the Constitution of the United States was adopted to secure domestic hostility. Under the constitution the people enjoyed the right to keep bare arms.

The American Spirit thrives on change. Change is that inescapable force that overcomes the inertia of complacency. The timeline of American achievement makes it clear that change has become the inevitable force that moved this country to its current place of dominance. It is easy to look at history from the perspective of a Monday-morning quarterback, who has the luxury to second-guess the change agents through instant replay.

As fascinating as the study of change can be, it is even more fascinating to consider visionary leaders who make change possible in our everyday experience. They are the ones who seem to understand the forces of human nature and know how to kindle the spark of change without being suffocated by fear.

Although the lessons we learn from past leaders are too numerous to list, a few notable examples come to mind, in the comfort of our homes and offices. Just think of the hardships overcome by George Washington at Valley Forge and the responsibility of being the first president of a country so fragile that its future was in doubt every day of his presidency. There were incredible contributions to a growing society from heroes like Franklin, Jefferson, and Jackson. Abraham Lincoln held the country together during its greatest internal conflict. When I think of change agents who made their mark on an entire country, I think of the impact of Henry Ford, Edison, and Carver. The leadership of Franklin Roosevelt brought to the country through the Great Depression and a world war. MacArthur, Eisenhower, Kennedy, and Reagan are just a few of the leaders who became synonymous with change. Whether their deeds are great or small, the records of successful leaders can help us emulate the best and try to improve the rest as we take on the challenges of implementing change.

From governmental service to corporate boardrooms, many gifted leaders have found the agony of defeat rather than the thrill of victory. Leaders come and go while new laws, plans, and policies fill volumes that gather dust on the shelves of would-be change agents—another new idea put to rest. How is it that some leaders turn failing organizations into harmonious entities celebrating victory? What is the formula they have learned that enables them to turn around organizations when others seem to spin their wheels as if stuck in the sands of the status quo? I believe they understand the human factor and are able to implement the technical aspects of the change process while involving the personnel who will be affected by the change.

We are about to see how the human factor can determine success or failure of a change effort. Policies are subject to situational demands and trends, but relationships last forever. Personal growth as a result of change can be a stimulating experience and something we look forward to. Even when needed, not all growth will be accepted or desired by those involved. It has been said that growth is the result of movement from a current condition to a more elevated level of existence. Those who experience the thrill of a harmonious working relationship have something special. For some reason, they get along well together and believe in a common cause. Their leaders are sensitive to the members of the team and bring its individuals together as a family. Human beings search for a positive environment; money can't buy it, and managers can't force it. It is all about supportive relationships perpetuated from within the organization.

Such a harmonious philosophy of leadership and change seems to be challenged by a Western philosophy of power leadership. Today we see power leaders building ever-stronger corporate positions and seeking ever-greater competitive advantages. Now, there is nothing wrong with seeking a competitive advantage. Competition is the essence of our market economy. Yet within organizations, it is the human factor that contributes to the development of a harmonious workforce; working relationships based upon it remain productive. Organizations that withstand the test of time do so by blending research, innovation, competition, and efficiency in a supportive team-oriented environment. The human factor is about the way we do business. In 1985, Roger Smith, the chairman of General Motors, was speaking on innovative systems regarding the Saturn product. I believe he understood the human factor when he asked, "Where is all this great stuff coming from? It's not really coming out of IBM. It's coming out of little two- and three-man companies because they're finding out that forty guys can't do something that three people can do. It's just the law of human nature" (Peters 1987, 239).

Too often I have observed educational leaders emulating corporate bottom-line philosophies and neglecting the human factor. Perhaps current political pressure from the data-driven accountability movement has caused some educators to overlook the equation that supports team-oriented problem solving in favor of a win-at-all-costs attitude.

By 1986 our elementary district had grown steadily over the years to three thousand students. The superintendent decided to expand the administrative team by creating an educational services coordinator. The new position would benefit the district by helping principals align curriculum to standards while providing needed staff development for teachers. The plan made sense, but any plan is only as good as the people involved. When Gerald Hopkins was introduced to the administrative council, the superintendent boldly predicted that Hopkins would take our curriculum "to the next level." As a new administrator, however, Hopkins didn't realize that the superintendent was under pressure from the board of trustees to improve scores and increase language acquisition for our growing Asian population. In other words, the superintendent was under the gun to bring results, and being a bottom-line guy, he had brought in Hopkins, who shared his management style.

I should have realized a new direction was on the way when the superintendent gave that introduction for Hopkins. "Taking performance to the next level" is a corporate cliché in leadership training, and as a new administrator, I bought it. Actually, it is arrogant to think that given the complexities of the educational arena one person can take an entire organization to a new level of performance. Educational leaders must always remember that the cornerstone of the educational process is the teacher. Teachers make the difference—through training in curriculum, instructional strategies, and learning styles. That evening at an administrative mixer, Don, the veteran principal in the district, whispered to me that he didn't see a red *S* on Hopkins's chest.

Don had become my unofficial mentor, and I remember questioning his sarcastic statement. After our first meeting with Hopkins, though, I discovered how prophetic Don's observation had been. At that time Don and I were leading the staff in a reform effort to turn the junior high into a middle school. Although the curriculum remained basically the same, the philosophy, instructional strategies, administrative scheduling, and intervention programs would see major changes for the veteran staff. Don understood the personalities of the staff and had orchestrated a plan to implement reform. He had sent a team of teachers to the National Middle School Conference in

Louisville, Kentucky, to learn about successful reform strategies. Through a series of planning sessions that followed, the school had reached consensus about its new direction. Once Don described our efforts to Hopkins, though, the conflict started.

"You can't build a sixth-grade core unless you create houses in separate locations on the campus," Hopkins quickly responded. "My last district tried to implement changes in just one year and it didn't work." Whether trying to impose his expertise or the authority of his newly established position, Hopkins was rich in killer phrases. By playing his old tapes—*We tried that and it didn't work,* and *You can't do it that way*—Hopkins inadvertently built a wall between the very factions he was there to unify. He just didn't understand the human factor of relationships. Fortunately for our staff, Don was a wily veteran administrator who listened cautiously and didn't overreact. Don had always told me that before you take action, get your ducks in line. I was about to see the master at work.

The following week Don moved quickly to schedule a meeting with the superintendent and Hopkins, but realizing that actual power comes from within the organization, he invited the entire staff as well. Knowing the strength and outgoing nature of the staff, Don intended to describe the plan in an open forum. He opened the meeting by thanking Hopkins for his suggestions and assuring him that the staff was excited about the new direction for the school. He had orchestrated the presentation so each department chair would report on various parts of the plan. The presentation was logical, student centered, and based on best practice. The staff was united and primed to describe what they had created. Not knowing the concerns raised earlier by Hopkins, the superintendent was impressed with the plan. Hopkins had no choice but to endorse the effort, declaring how pleased he was to be a part of the reform effort.

From that moment on, Hopkins kept his distance from our school, concentrating his efforts on the elementary schools. At administrative council meetings he treaded cautiously around Don. From that experience I learned that change is not about winning or losing but about unifying and coming together for a common cause and getting ducks in line.

If the Western formula for corporate leadership is dominated by a bottom-line philosophy of competition, power, speed, and profit, where do individuals fit in? Has education, in adopting the corporate bottom-line philosophy, moved too far in objective analysis of human data without regard for the values of building stable relationships? In what direction are the federal and state education dollars flowing? For some districts the question may actually be whether dollars are flowing at all.

Historically, leaders can be defined by their practice of the "power triad." Whether in the governmental, corporate, or institutional arenas, decisions are influenced by a triad of *knowledge, force,* and *finance.* Throughout history, human interactions have been influenced by one element of the triad or combinations of them. However, does the power triad bring wisdom to an organization? Not necessarily. History teaches that power is ultimately defeated yet wisdom endures the test of time. So why aren't our leaders being trained in wisdom? Perhaps wisdom surrenders to expedience in the high-pressure business of American public education. Leaders come in a variety of styles, and all bring their versions of change to their organizations. In the face of time lines and district-level pressure, authoritative direction is faster than building relationships that enable collective decisions. Can a self-centered or ruthless leader bring positive change to an organization? The answer is yes, but at what cost? How are relationships affected? Will the change be sustainable? Usually such change efforts last only as long as the leaders that enforced them.

In *The Prince* (written in 1513 and published in 1532), Machiavelli discusses the relevance of leadership in the context of moral and expedient decisions of sixteenth-century Italy. Over the centuries the book has become essential reading for leadership training. Knowledge, force, and finance affect twenty-first-century decisions just as they did in the time of Machiavelli. Through the trials of the Medici era of Florence, Machiavelli came to a variety of conclusions about how leaders influence and rule. He discovered that leaders who adjust to the circumstances of the time will find success. Further, leaders who act with compassionate authority will prosper more than those who remain timid and reactive (Adams 1992, 117). Such lessons from Machiavelli are not too distant to have practical applications for school leaders seeking change in today's environment.

One of the benefits of the emerging global economy is the infusion of Eastern thought into Western management style. Perhaps the blending of management philosophies from different cultures will help define the leadership strategies for the twenty-first century. Effective leaders keep searching for better ways to get the job done. In 1986, Don wasn't aware of Eastern managerial strategies or the writings of Machiavelli when he led a school reform movement. He just understood and respected people, and his methods made sense, so people felt confidence in the new direction.

Modern China is rapidly taking its place in the world market partly because of a management style that is consistent with its historical culture. The ancient Chinese philosophy of virtue and reciprocity is still practiced by modern Chinese managers. The concept of *Quan Xi* emphasizes the importance of honor in business and personal relationships. In China, confrontational management styles based on pressure to perform are replaced with mutual trust and reciprocity. To receive, we must first give.

Business accountability in China is still a direct result of adherence to *Quan Xi*. When one is delegated a task. one is held accountable for the quality of the result. When needed, correction is given through a deductive approach, bringing insight to the employee without loss of face. China's ancient book of wisdom, the *I Ching*, teaches that the leader must respect the natural laws of governing: "Just as the wind causes the grass to sway, a wise man inspires those who hear him" (Ho 1986, 101). There is a profound difference between inspiring and forcing. True leaders guide fellow workers to aspire to collective goals through accepted expectations.

Don't be misled into believing that this ancient management style has applications only to seemingly high-powered corporate managers. The lessons from the global economy are reaching all the way into local schools. With the integration of multiple cultures into American educational system, today's leaders are utilizing skills that demonstrate the strength of diversity. School leaders are facing the challenges of the global society within their own schools. I know of schools in California where sixty-three languages are spoken; administrators there find the task of locating qualified teachers more than just an academic challenge but a matter of survival. Teachers from diverse backgrounds require training to meet the academic and social needs of children as schools become mini-global communities. One district sought to improve staff diversity by recruiting teachers from the Philippines, only to find that social and cultural differences created a new set of challenges for foreign-trained teachers. The Filipino teachers quickly found that American students demonstrated an entirely different level of respect for teachers than what they were used to.

It stands to reason that in education, systemic changes are built from within. By establishing meaningful problem-solving teams, teachers are soon brought to realize that they are not token participants of a top-down change effort. Throughout history, political revolutions grew from the people. Many revolutions have taken place without all three aspects of the power triad, but over time the elements of the triad surfaced as the rebellions strengthened. Whether on the scale of historic change in a global sense or the efforts of a local school attempting to do something different, the lessons are the same. When leaders can create effective teams where people are supported and treated with respect, change becomes systemic.

Within the context of our multicultural society, educators face the challenges of developing programs that bring academic proficiency to all children. Most states are creating standardized testing plans designed to measure academic standards, and some administrators face enormous pressure to raise test scores. There is so much pressure, in fact, that in some states after two years of underachievement principals can be removed and teachers reassigned, to improve the system. In some cases meaningful classes have been eliminated to make room for more remediation. One district in California has eliminated elective courses in its middle school and high school in order to provide more reading and math classes. Think of it—children with an average attention span of twelve minutes attending school for six hours a day concentrating solely on reading and math. The absence of such project-based electives as band, choir, or shop classes creates a void in a child's educational environment. Is this an example of bottom-line management based on data-driven decisions? A total evaluation of a child's growth requires both objective as well as subjective data. The problem in obtaining an accurate evaluation is that overworked and overstressed educators find objective data easier to obtain.

There is no question that the public wants education to be accountable and that in many cases reading and math scores need to improve. Wouldn't it make more sense if schools focused on teaching children, while recognizing that each child has a multitude of needs beyond reading and math? Yes, we need to improve reading and math, but let's not forget the rest of the child. Many districts have improved test scores by restructuring academic programs, starting in the early grades. If California is an example of our new multicultural society, schools face enormous challenges, and not just in reading and math. The civic virtues of tolerance, respect, and responsibility are in short supply in many schools. Remember Columbine? Recently California authorities uncovered a plot by eight students planning a mass murder of African American students in their high school. I recently sat on an expulsion panel for a Pakistani student who had attacked a boy who had made fun of his religion. What can schools do to instill civic virtues of tolerance, respect, and responsibility?

Values are first taught in the home. All too often schools must reshape the teaching of the family. Our schools are obligated to uphold the Constitution as states and local school boards establish policies that are consistent with the law. One program that has met with much success in high schools across the nation is Civic Education, developed by the Center for Civic Education. This congressionally funded program has had an immediate impact in the schools that have used the curriculum. Students learn that civic virtue is part of everyday life. Speaking of data-driven decisions, studies have shown that 82 percent of those who have gone through the program have taken upon themselves the responsibility to vote, as opposed to just 48 percent of their peers. Students who have gone through Civic Education have an increased understanding of the Constitution and the Bill of Rights, as well as greater political tolerance than the average American. Educators are creative people, and as long as there is a need, talented teachers will develop programs like Civic Education to meet the needs of our children.

In California, the middle-school document *Caught in the Middle* outlines the importance of teaching the whole child. Academic standards and instructional exemplars provide templates upon which schools can create balanced education. Whether in elementary, middle, or high schools, children have unique needs that schools must recognize. In fact, schools must do more than recognize the needs of their children, they must teach to them. This concept is even more important in our emerging global community. Schools can't educate alone; parents have the responsibility to reinforce classroom lessons through meaningful study at home.

Steven Covey (1990) writes about getting our priorities in order, in *Principle-Centered Leadership:* "But if we learn to manage things and lead people we will have the best bottom line because we will unleash the energy and talent of people" (p. 17). In 1954, behavioral scientist Abraham Maslow published his "hierarchy of needs," a general pattern of needs recognition (see table 3.1). He theorized that a person must satisfy current needs before realizing higher ones. His work identifies the root causes behind our decisions. Often unrecognized, our physiological needs determine our responses to external stimuli.

Let's apply these principles to the change process. An individual will not seek self-actualization until his or her basic needs of self-preservation and security have been met. Basic needs must be satisfied before moving up the scale. This could be a primary reason why life in many third-world countries, torn by terrorism, struggles for dominance, and greed, is still a struggle. Basic physiological needs must be filled before esteem and self-actualization can be sought.

In the workplace the need for safety, which is manifested through security and stability, creates a natural barrier to change. Just think of an organization where employees who are satisfied with their present condition receive a change of direction from new management. Suddenly, homeostasis is disturbed. A natural rebellion can occur, a tug-of-war. Each faction holds on to one end of the rope; as one side pulls, the other pulls harder, thereby creating resistance.

What if leaders recognized Maslow's principles and actually used them to create effective change? After all, it is the leader's responsibility to be sure that the first two levels, physiological and safety, are in place before building on the natural feelings of belonging, esteem, and self-actualization. Once again, we see that such a model is dependent upon trust and shared belief in a common cause.

Systemic change requires collaboration and consideration of the needs of others. In service organizations, respect and trust narrows the gap between management and labor. Interest-based negotiations, as opposed to adversarial bargaining, can focus on issues instead of personalities in order to bring opposing sides closer to the middle.

Table 3.1. Maslow's Hierarchy of Needs (Gawel 1997, 2)

Level	Type of Need	Examples
1	Physiological	Thirst, sex, hunger
2	Safety	Security, stability, protection
3	Love and belonging	Gaining a sense of belonging
4	Esteem	Self-respect/respect for others
5	Self-actualization	Fulfilling one's potential

Our district policy called for administrators to participate in the negotiation process. I have many fond memories serving on the administrator's classified and certified negotiating teams for several years. Well, at least I have memories of serving in the team. Like many other districts, we had practiced adversarial bargaining until a new spirit of interest-based negotiations took hold. Both sides went through the training with outward smiles, amid light-hearted relationship-building activities. Some called it "touchy-feely" training. Then it came time to gather around the table. Now, for a district that had been used to adversarial negotiations for years to concentrate suddenly on issues and not personalities seemed like filling a swimming pool with a spoon. It started slowly.

There are different reasons why people serve on negotiation teams. For some it's an ego trip; others feel they are acting as a watchdog to protect the rights of employees from greedy management. On the management side egos are definitely involved as well, and some feel they are protecting the district from greedy employees always wanting more. For me, negotiations were like being a football coach. You have to be smart enough to understand the game and dumb enough to think it's important.

To ensure that the first sessions were on target, the superintendent brought in a consultant to keep both sides focused on the issues. By the end of the second day we had progressed through the contract and had come to the issue of the time-out room. At my school we had created a time-out room where disruptive students were sent to complete assignments. Students remained in the room for a period, then returned to their other classes. It was sort of a safety valve that supported our new discipline policy. Students were held accountable by having to complete reading, writing, and math assignments. All was well with the program until the classified team expressed the concerns that the time-out room was too far from the office and the clerk was not credentialed and should be supervising students. The management team's position was that the room was in a portable building adjacent to the office and that the clerk worked under the supervision of the credentialed administrators. At that moment the process could have easily focused on personalities and degenerated into a power struggle.

Thanks to the skill of the consultant, both sides listed the issues. Our consultant helped both sides clarify the issues and then guided the problem-solving process as we discussed solutions. Then Ellen, the president of the classified association, came up with an idea. (Ellen had been president for some time and had a reputation as a tough negotiator. She had recently been transferred to my school as the health clerk, and I found her to be very logical and fair.) Now, it so happened that I was planning to remodel the office. The staff had outgrown the small staff room, which also served as a teacher work room. The plan would move a class out of a connected room, and open the wall to create a new staff room, work room, and conference room. What, she suggested, if we turned the old staff room into a new time-out room and redesigned the new rooms to include a smaller work room, a new staff room, and a conference room? Her solution was interest basing at its best. I quickly sketched out a rough floor plan and realized it could work. The new time-out room would be next door to the vice principal, solving the issue of proximity and supervision. The two sides had worked together; both had focused on issues and realized that the other could contribute to a solution. What an attitude adjustment! It was a very positive experience that demonstrated that change can be in the best interest of all concerned. Our agreement did wonders for the relationship between the management and the classified team during the following months.

What can our nation's history teach us about the fundamentals of change? Is change permanent? It is interesting to discover that history reveals change as dependent upon the social forces existing at a given time. Is it possible that decisions made in one period may be deemed unacceptable in another? Consider the decisions formed in our country just a few years after victory in the war for independence. Our young nation believed that expansion was its birthright. Manifest Destiny became a badge of legitimacy, the expression of an appetite for new territory that could only be satisfied through expansion. The dynamics of American expansion reveal the glory that was then associated with exploration, whatever the expense to those who were there first. The Mexicans of California and Texas and the Native Americans of the plains viewed American expansion in a different light. Theirs was a story of life trampled by the American quest for more. Romantic yet tragic, their sad story of subjugation and displacement was overshadowed by the thrill of victory for a growing nation. The challenges faced by the victorious and the vanquished are repeated throughout the history of the world.

Not even a hundred years would pass from the signing of the Declaration of Independence before our nation's sixteenth president would declare, "In giving freedom to the slave, we assure freedom to the free, honorable alike in what we give and what we preserve" (National Archives and Records Administration 2003, Abraham Lincoln). Lincoln spoke of change, but change was not universally accepted in the 1860s.

Can change be forced on people who are unwilling to move? We would do well to remember the lessons history has taught us about control and dominance through the ages. From kings and queens to dictators and despots, we have learned that enduring change comes from an inner spirit, not from external force. Can the human heart be forced to comply with what is contrary to its origin whatever the prevailing justification? Can coercion and fear bring immediate change? Probably, but such change usually lasts only as long as the power that initiated it in the first place. History reveals that such change implementation strategies will not endure.

The fact that even our elected leaders are mere mortals is reflected in a long history of conflicting decisions made under the pressure of the moment. Considered a dark day in American jurisprudence, when the Supreme Court rendered a decision that would not only divide a country but form an impression of doubt that has remained for many to this day. It was March 6, 1857, when Chief Justice Roger Taney read a majority opinion that black people were not citizens. The Dred Scott decision asserted that that group could not expect protection from the federal government or the courts (National Archives and Records Administration 2003, Dred Scott).

It did not take long for pressure to mount. Ultimately that decision was overturned by the Thirteenth and Fourteenth Amendments to the Constitution. On June 13, 1866, the new amendments were passed:

All persons born or naturalized in the United States, and subject to the jurisdiction thereof, are citizens of the United States and of the state where they reside. No State shall make or enforce any law which shall abridge the privileges or immunities of citizens of the United States; nor shall any State deprive any person of life, liberty, or property, without due process of law; nor deny to any person within its jurisdiction the equal protection of the law. (National Archives and Records Administration 2003, The Constitution: Amendments 14)

Social pressures for the prohibition of alcohol, considered just at the time, forced passage of the Eighteenth Amendment in 1919. By 1933 circumstances had changed, and the Eighteenth Amendment was repealed by the Twenty-First Amendment. Time is measured in swings of the pendulum.

Change falls hard on those who are not ready or willing. What is the natural reaction when people are forced to do something contrary to their beliefs? They will resist and pull back from the unknown, seeking the comfort of what is known. Effective leaders recognize the rebellious side of human nature and can adapt change efforts accordingly.

It is obvious that some political decisions cannot stand the test of time. Decisions that have forced the separation of people based upon race or sex were subject to prevailing philosophies. It wasn't until 1919 that the Nineteenth Amendment brought full rights to women. After lifetimes of trial and pain, the women's suffrage movement was finally victorious. It is even more astonishing how slow the acceptance of this change was. Maryland did not ratify the amendment until 1941 and didn't transmit its ratification to the State Department until 1958.

In 1973, the legal framework once again attempted to change behavior when the Supreme Court rendered the famed *Roe vs. Wade* decision. The issue of personal rights was challenged in 1970 when Jane Roe filed suit against Dallas County over its interpretation of legalized abortion. The results of that decision forced states to change their individual abortion laws, a change that has had bitter consequences for many. Time will tell whether the tide of public sentiment will change that decision also.

Our brief look at change and government further reveals how the United States has continued to mold its personality through struggle and triumph. Before America celebrated its two-hundredth anniversary, it had been changed forever by the industrial revolution and had survived the trials of the Civil War, the mobilization of its people in World War I, and an economic depression that eventually led to a national transformation of lifestyle. A new sense of unity during World War II demonstrated how the individual, business, and governmental sectors could mobilize their efforts toward a common cause. The exhilaration of a space race in the shadows of a cold war followed, and then the struggle for basic human rights at home in the 1960s.

We have seen a segregated society trapped in endless frustration evolve into urban anarchy fed by civil disobedience in the 1960s. Vietnam and Watergate in the 1970s changed the way our nation viewed its government. It was a time when any establishment became fair game for public scrutiny;

speculation and hidden agendas became synonymous with government. Today, the escalation of the illegal drug industry threatens the very desires that once conceived an age of experimentation. The international drug culture has become so dominant that governments are forced to negotiate terms for mutual existence with drug cartels. An epidemic of anarchy by today's urban gangs threatens to overwhelm the very spirit of due process. Even gangsters promote the change process through their violent lifestyle. Governments, communities, and schools are forced to change policies in order to counter the effects of gang activity. Some citizens of battle-torn inner-city neighborhoods ask if there is any hope. If history is our teacher, the answer is yes, because all things are subject to change. Change is the only constant in the human experience. You can count on it. However, the time it takes for change to take place and the methods used to bring it about are as unpredictable and inconsistent as the legislation we have just reviewed. There is one thing we can be sure of, and that is that change will happen. The hope for civilized people everywhere is that change will improve and protect the quality of life.

It seems logical to assume that by understanding the process of change and the attributes of human nature, we can better understand how to implement desirable change within our organizations. The fundamentals of the human spirit exist in all organizations, regardless of their size or purpose. As we look back and focus our global microscope of time, we see people trying to change their environment through various means. History documents change efforts manifested through rebellion, dominance, pride, and envy. Whatever the culture, a close examination of human endeavors reveals the universal desire for independence. Slaves want freedom, and conquered people crave independence. Current levels of individual satisfaction eventually give way to desires for more. Of course, some cultures exhibit this characteristic to a greater degree than others, but history shows how people strive for what they believe is a better life. The records of antiquity also reveal how the forces of complacency can block the path of change, just as the quest for independence can be suppressed by a myriad of torturous means. Understanding the psychological reasons why people choose to dominate each other can reveal effective strategies that leaders can use to bring desired change rather than force change through dominance. The challenge for leaders is to uncover the reason why people act the way they do—not an easy task but one that will bring enlightenment to the decision-making process.

How will history judge our time? If rational consideration for the welfare of others is the measure, the actions of many of our world leaders demonstrate how little the human experience has evolved. There are still more people on this planet who are dominated by self-serving philosophies than those who are free to choose their own directions in life. While some governments recognize the individual worth of their citizens, many regimes subscribe to philosophies of suppression and dominance. For such cultures, very little has changed over thousands of years. Terrorism has resurfaced, as the word of fear for this new century. The U.S. State Department has identified well-known terrorist governments in the world, listing seven to be the most active: within Iran, Sudan, Cuba, Iraq, Libya, North Korea, and Syria, thirty-six individual groups are determined to make changes in the world through terror (U.S. State Department 2002, Thinkquest.org.). Even after the fall of Saddam Hussein's Iraq, factional terrorists tainted the joys of the people who momentarily experienced freedom from oppression. Terrorists are change agents in their own right, but their methods are not consistent with documented systemic change strategies. History has proven that forcible coercion may produce short-term change but that the innate flame of individual liberty will eventually overcome coercion. Unfortunately, the only positive changes the subjugated masses can experience are in their dreams. This scenario is not limited to international politics; I think of a dictatorial school principal who attempted to force his will on a staff in the name of change.

Some say our nation is turning to the corporate god of greed while privately reaching up from the depths of daily routines just to touch the pinnacle of fantasy. We envy those who have more and idolize those who seemingly have it all. Many Americans pay millions to people who will teach them how to change. Many believe that their favorite celebrities have found enlightenment and can advise them on all aspects of life. From toothpaste to political interpretations, millions line up for advice.

For better or worse, our personal action plans for success require that we change from our current condition. We all dream. It's good to dream. Some of us actually follow our dreams, by making a plan. Then there are those who boldly take the first step on a quest for something new. Leaders who understand the spirit of change that burns within all humans will have a clearer insight into how the human factor can make or break their change efforts.

II

THE PROCESS
OF CHANGE

4

WHY ME?

Standing in the middle of the road is very dangerous; you get knocked down by the traffic from both sides.

—Margaret Thatcher

Why should I get involved in change effort? After all, there are always risks with any change. In the world of sports, the coach is the first one blamed when things go wrong. As a new teacher, I saw principals arrive full of enthusiasm only to be crushed by a dominating staff determined to resist any direction other than their own. It was then that I learned about controlling personalities. As a principal, I've seen fellow administrators lose reputations for credibility in a moment of indecision. At the high school level, there are all the games and activities to supervise as well as complaining parents to confront. Principals have enough to do just to exist from day to day. The administrator's agenda grows longer every year—the nagging demands of public education to do more with less. A week in the life of a principal could very well cover gang awareness activities, special education individual education plan (IEP) meetings, administrative council meetings, noon supervision, standardized test preparation, lesson plan reviews, teacher evaluations, afternoon parent meetings, night game supervision, a 504 behavior-modification meeting, a board meeting at night, a parent complaint, staff bickering, purchase orders to complete—and somehow the principal must find time to be a visionary leader for the school and a mentor for the teachers. A balanced diet for school administrators is often coffee in one hand and a cookie in the other during noon supervision. There were times when I cursed the inventor of voice mail. It's tough to get away and totally clear your mind of business. One clue that you need to get away is when you start to look like the picture on your driver's license. When I think about it, why would anyone want to go through the scrutiny of being a school administrator?

I believe the answer lies deep within each one of us. Are you driven, or are you called? A driven person is intensely committed to achieving a goal and willing to utilize all of the resources available. Driven to achieve, these people are relentless in the pursuit of achievement and will go over, around, or through any obstacle that stands in their way. Some of our best leaders are driven to achieve excellence. "Called" leaders possess the same passion as those who are driven but feel a vocation to social responsibility pulling them forward. Called leaders, who are deeply committed to helping society, often live by a strong spiritual system of values. Ken Blanchard speaks of the value of conviction in both coaching and life: "I believe that genuine faith is eminently practical, and that a vast resource for inner knowing stands ready to assist today's leader who will try it" (Blanchard and Shula 1995, 39).

We all have a different reason for being, and I have found that called leaders live by a set of values that give them strength to weather the storms of criticism strongly associated with leadership. They do the right things for the right reasons. Regardless of one's inner passion for success, all leaders must live by high standards of character if they are to be successful over the long haul. We all know of castle climbers who drive to the top just to leap into new challenges. It seems that the true test of leadership is the test of time. Have lives changed for the better because of your actions? Character is doing the right thing when no one is looking. Do you still get a thrill from making a difference in a youngster's life? What do you feel when your efforts energize an employee caught in the doldrums of mid-career repetition? These are time-tested, life-changing experiences that define our leadership styles. In his book *Everyone's a Coach*, Don Shula, the legendary coach of the Miami Dolphins, speaks about that special conviction successful leaders possess: "The problem with most leaders today is they don't stand for anything. Leadership implies movement toward something, and convictions provide that direction. If you don't stand for something, you'll fall for anything" (Blanchard and Shula 1995, 27).

I remember a moment just three weeks before our first graduation; it is lodged in my memory forever. The seniors were excited about the big event. I had worked with parents who were planning a ceremony that would set the standard for years to come. It had been a year of firsts for our new high school. The first senior class had overcome the challenges of opening a new school and was about to graduate. The school culture had taken a quantum leap forward, and it was riding the crest of positive energy from an unde-feated, championship football season. Corporate scholarships were over-whelming for a first graduating class. Yet amid the excitement of the year-end activities, it was one quiet moment that told the story of people committed to each other.

Have you ever met someone who has become the lifeblood of an organiza-tion, someone who gives off such positive energy that their caring spirit touches whomever they come in contact with? Truly genuine people don't plan it, it just happens. Carol Nicolas was such a person. As a parent, she never missed an opportunity to serve the school. From boosters, fund-raising, and parent-teacher associations to her endless donation of ideas and time, she had been instrumental in shaping the support system for the new school. Fi-nally, assuming the position of office clerk, she fittingly coordinated student body activities and budgets as programs continued to grow. The position was perfect for Carol. Now she could still support the school and at the same time be close to her twin senior boys. Like any proud parent, she eagerly antici-pated their graduation in June.

Shortly before Christmas break, however, Carol didn't seem to be herself. Though still positive in her relationships, she looked tired. We all said that the break would help her get some needed rest, and no one gave it much thought. Not even in January, when school resumed but she didn't return, did anyone see a cause for concern; she had called to say she would be visit-ing her sister in Colorado for a few weeks. In any busy organization, the hec-tic pace turns days into weeks as people adjust to personnel changes, and life goes on.

In early March, Carol returned, and the now-growing speculations were answered. She attempted to resume her responsibilities of student-body clerk, but it soon became obvious that her health was failing fast. Carol had cancer. The disease had progressed rapidly, and the prognosis was terminal. After three courageous weeks, she was unable to keep up with the pressures of the position, and she returned home to rest. We didn't see much of Carol during the next two months, as she preferred to keep to herself at home. In early June family members began arriving, and their reports were tragic. We were about to face a challenge that would test our courage and compassion. Carol's dream was to see her two children graduate from the new high school, but doctors had informed the family that the end was near, that she would not make it to graduation on the seventh of June.

This brings me to that moment. How could we give something back to someone who had given so much? There is always a way. Knowing that time was running out, family, friends, and the school worked feverishly to create a graduation ceremony three weeks before the real event. The day finally arrived, in room 412 at Mercy Hospital. For the few of us in attendance, it would be a graduation ceremony unlike any we had experienced. The time had come; everyone was in place. I reached down to turn on the tape player, and the somber melody of "Pomp and Circumstance" filled the room. There was Carol lying on her side in her bed, her sister kneeling next to her describing in whispers what was taking place. At that moment, Bill and Bryce ceremoniously walked into the room wearing their deep red graduation robes and caps. The two boys stopped just in front of Carol's bed. I turned off the music; a brief graduation address was read, and diplomas were presented to each boy. We all applauded their accomplishment as Carol's sister knelt closer still whispering a description of the beautiful ceremony. The boys knelt in front of their mother and gave her a big hug. Tears filled the room amid feelings of pride on behalf of one who had given so much. Though so young, Carol's sons displayed unusual courage and never broke down as their small procession proudly marched out of the room to music. I'll never know how much of that ceremony Carol was aware of, but it truly brought people together for a common cause.

But some will ask, Why me? Why should I take on the burden and responsibilities of leadership? I can only think of one simple answer. You'll never really understand until you've been there. When you believe that leadership is a privilege and feel the satisfaction of working with people and in some small way helping them make life better for others, then you will understand the essence of leadership.

Is it safe and politically correct to follow a status-quo style of change? Is that statement an oxymoron? Isn't the status quo the opposite of change?

Here I refer to "status-quo change" as a conservative version of leadership. Such a style of leadership holds onto the present and implements subtle changes as each crisis dictates. But being reactive rather than proactive is not true leadership.

Where is the passion for the cause when leaders concentrate on the safety of their current situations and then join popular opinion to manage a crisis that could have been prevented with a proactive approach? The symbiotic relationship between leadership and management is fundamental to the change process. You can't have one without the other. Leadership provides the blueprint, management brings the tools, and with both the job gets done.

Leaders who make a difference are those who are willing to take a stand for what they believe is the best solution for their organizations. It is through true leadership that the human factor is revealed. Educational institutions exist for the purpose of providing academic and social education for children. Without being overly dramatic, it must be said that our society as we know it hangs in the balance of each generation we educate. Passionate leaders are committed to a vision to ensuring that every child has maximum opportunities for success. Educators who carry such a vision see a battle raging for the minds of young people. Today's youth find growing up hard enough by itself without the tantalizing influences of self-indulgence and peer pressure. Young minds are bombarded by messages that can lead to self-destruction. If you question the seriousness of the negative forces influencing youth, take a walk down the isle of your local video store and observe the messages displayed. Leadership in education today is more than charting test results for demographic subgroups.

What do twelve-year-olds care about academic standards when they have other worries? Some are worried about whether they can eat without being threatened for their lunch money. Others are worried about which way to walk home after school, because those guys dressed in red are always hanging around. Some worry that stray gunshots at night may miss their marks. Maybe worst of all is that some night their real father will reenter, bringing back all that pain. An eleven-year-old boy once told me that his headaches went away after his father went away. A junior in college tells the story of finally getting away from home when he transferred to an out-of-state university. He remembers that his first nights sleeping in his dorm room were filled with nightmares of his father stomping through their house in a drunken rage. It would take years for those painful memories to fade. These are the issues teachers face in their classrooms every day. To meet the needs of their clients, leaders must understand the forces that influence youth culture.

Before the change process even begins, someone must make a commitment to take on a process that may invariably alienate half of those involved. Change can be painful and unsettling. "The key to success in the school is the principal principle," said Jane Eisner in the conclusion of her research on effective schools (DuFour and Eaker 1992, 42). Peal (1986) states how the law of supply can influence a committed leader: personal good will flow abundantly when it is not blocked by negative thought and action (p. 105). In *The Power of Ethical Management,* Blanchard and Peale (1998) speak of a personal desire to seek meaning and definition in life, of how the desire to seek purpose is ongoing (p. 44).

In his book *Winning Every Day,* Lou Holtz (1998) describes ten steps he believes affect individual decisions about the future:

- The power of attitude
- Taking on adversity
- Having a sense of purpose
- Willing to sacrifice
- Learning to adapt to the situation
- Chasing your dreams
- Nurturing your self-image
- Building trust
- Committing to excellence
- Treating others as you would be treated. (p. xiv)

Not all leaders are willing to take on a change effort. Some leaders must have the strength to be an individual while understanding that when things go wrong, people will blame the leader. By blaming their leaders in difficult times, people tend to feel released from their responsibilities. Yet some people strive on pressure. I've often thought that if it weren't for stress, I'd have no energy at all. It is interesting that the model in Japan is different; there the group realizes that it is their job to solve problems for the leader.

A reason leaders stand up for reform could be to satisfy the human need for recognition. The Peters and Waterman study in 1982 described the desire of an individual to be part of a winning team (DuFour and Eaker 1992, 27). Their work also found that at the foundation of the most successful companies in our country was the concept of a winning team. Their research discovered that just as in athletics, winning performances become contagious. By continuously celebrating winning when it occurs, organizations are able to keep the momentum going.

In his book *The Fifth Discipline,* Peter Senge (Kleiner et al. 1994) asks, Why bother? The personal energy required to lead a change effort can seem overwhelming. When it comes to personal commitment, he cites the comments of Konosuke Matsushita, the innovative creator of Masushita of Japan, who believes that his purpose is to help every individual within his organization achieve superior economic performance. Senge also describes how good the CEO of Xerox Canada, David McCamus, felt when his efforts ultimately led to satisfied customers.

In his book *The 7 Habits of Highly Effective People,* Steven Covey (1990a) illustrates how some people gain self-satisfaction by breaking with tradition and seeing things in a new light. He lists the work of Thomas Kuhn, known for introducing the term "paradigm shift" in his *The Structure of Scientific Revolutions.* Kuhn argues that almost every major scientific breakthrough was the result of someone breaking the old paradigm and looking at things in a new way (Covey 1990a, 29). Leaders who are able to orchestrate the change of culture within an organization have themselves undergone personal transformations. Trustworthiness is the fundamental principle of leadership.

I have always been fascinated by the leadership displayed by outstanding coaches. People who are able to withstand the pressures of the arena live by their convictions and can still be successful. In *They Call Me Coach,* John Wooden (1972) spoke of the importance of personal commitment and the desire to care for others. He said that coaches must regard their responsibility as a sacred trust, because of the many lives that are influenced by their actions (p. 99). Finally, coach Mike Krzyzewski (2000), in light of his years of collegiate success, writes of his passion that led him to work in the pressure-filled world of college basketball: "My passion is to coach and do things to the best of my ability. If we can do that, the other stuff will take care of itself" (p. 54).

In light of these inspirational examples, the answer to the opening question seems clear. Leaders who get involved in change efforts do so because they live by the conviction of their passion. Educational leaders realize that their job will never be done until every child within their organization experiences maximum opportunities for success. There can be no half-hearted existence for the leader committed to excellence. Everyone dreams, but it's the effective leaders who work to make their dreams become reality. In *I Could Do Anything If I Only Knew What It Was,* Barbara Sher wrote of accomplishing dreams: "You must go after your wish. As soon as you start to pursue a dream, your life wakes up and everything has meaning" (Motivationalquotes.com, Sher).

For every negative impression that evolves from our educational system there is positive wisdom that helps to bring disappointment into perspective. Although at times positive perspectives can be difficult to find once we step into the arena. I can assure you they do exist. Once there was a teaching applicant who felt a new sense of dedication and in the middle of a high-tech career chose to become a teacher. It had been years since he had attended a public school, and after reading the list of challenges awaiting his arrival he drafted a response to his principal.

> Let me see if I have this right. You want me to go into a room with all those kids and every fifty minutes a new group comes in my room, that's 150 a day. You expect me to fill their day with a love for learning. I'm supposed to instill a sense of pride in their ethnicity, behaviorally modify disruptive behavior, observe them for signs of abuse and T-shirt messages. I am to fight the war on drugs and sexually transmitted diseases, check their backpacks for guns and raise their self-esteem. I'm to teach them patriotism, good citizenship, sportsmanship and fair play, how and where to register to vote, how to balance a checkbook and how to apply for a job. I am to check their heads occasionally for lice, maintain a safe environment, recognize signs of potential antisocial behavior, offer advice, write letters of recommendation for student employment and scholarships, encourage respect for the cultural diversity of others, and, oh yes, always make sure that I give the girls in my class 50 percent of my attention. I'm required by my contract to be working on my own time, summer and evenings at my own expense toward advance certification and a master's degree; and after school, I am to attend committee and faculty meetings and participate in staff development and training to maintain my employment status. I am to be a shining example of virtue in such a way that my very presence will motivate my students to be obedient and respectful of authority. I am to pledge allegiance, without a flag, to support family values, to return to the basics, and

be loyal to my current administration. I am to incorporate technology into the learning with one computer. You expect me to monitor all Web sites while providing a personal relationship with each student. I am to decide who might be potentially dangerous and/or liable to commit crimes in school or who is possibly being abused, and I can be sent to jail for not mentioning these suspicions. I am to make sure all students pass the state and federally mandated testing and all classes, whether or not they attend school on a regular basis or complete any of the work assigned. Plus, I am expected to make sure that all of the students with handicaps are guaranteed a free and equal education, regardless of their mental or physical handicap. I am to communicate frequently with each student's parent by letter, phone, newsletter and progress report At 3:30 in the afternoon I'm to escort female teachers in my room area off campus because teachers not allowed on campus after hours for security reasons. I'm to do all of this with just minimal training, a marker and white board, a computer, a class set of books, a bulletin board, a 45-minute plan time and a big smile, all on a starting salary just twice that of the national poverty level that qualifies my family for food stamps in many states. Is that all?

And you want me to do all of this and expect me not to pray?

No wonder we see such high teacher dropout rates within the first five years of initial employment. It takes a special person to become a teacher—one who can climb out of the arena and maintain a dedication to help children.

So, Why me? The answer can be summarized with the response, Why *not* me? I like Greg Anderson's statement in his *The 22 Non-Negotiable Laws of Wellness:* "Let us be about setting high standards for life, love, creativity and wisdom. If our expectations in these areas are low, we are not likely to experience wellness. Setting high standards makes every day and every decade worth looking forward to" (Motivationalquotes.com, Anderson).

My research of award-winning schools tells me that 82 percent of leaders questioned indicated they had extensive or considerable commitment to personally assuming the challenge of change. That passion to make a difference in education became evident when I asked leaders why they personally took on the challenge of change:

- To improve student achievement
- I wanted to make difference
- It's my job to lead

- I had the credibility to lead
- A strong desire to build a high-functioning team
- Because the previous administration was not successful
- Believed in supporting individual dreams of accomplishment

The evidence continues to mount that we should never lose sight of the fact that education is first and foremost a people business. Bringing about change can be a struggle as well as a labor of love. What was rewarding for those who completed the process? One study indicates that staff enthusiasm was most important. Change is implemented through the people within the organization. Programs, policies, and test scores were not, I have found, the driving forces behind many successful change agents. I also found that educational leaders recognize the human factor as the essential element of the change process. Award-winning schools found that overall staff satisfaction to be the most rewarding result of their change efforts (Zimbalist 2001, 72).

- Staff enthusiasm
- Increased staff morale
- Positive energy among the staff
- Praise from individuals within the organization
- Student success
- Strong camaraderie within the staff
- Happy students and parents
- The change in attitude in the school culture
- Parent satisfaction
- Results
- A smoothly running organization
- Improved test scores

I have become a believer in that old saying, "Life is too short." When I was first married, I couldn't even relate to that wisdom. The day at hand was full of its own excitement, and the future was for some other time. Those who spent hours planning for the future were guys who sat in front of desks wearing suits, selling insurance. Being a product of the late 1960s, I too was caught up in the antiestablishment era. The last thing I would ever expect was a career where I would have to wear a tie every day. As a freshman in college, however, I experienced one of those life-changing moments. An architecture major, I thought I was pretty good at designing and creating, and I was looking forward to a career as an architect. Then one day our class went on a field trip to a large architectural firm. I saw a long corridor of small cubicles filled with early-career architects working on plans. Suddenly I had a flashback to the prison scene from Alexandre Dumas's *The Count of Monte Cristo.* Now I realize that I was taking a narrow view of the scene, but at the time I perceived a lack of freedom that was stifling. That was it for my architectural career. The next week I changed my major to education, with great plans on coaching. I didn't exactly know why, but I longed for a people-oriented career—a career filled with challenges and great causes.

Time and circumstances change attitudes and confirm convictions. As I gained leadership opportunities over the years, I began to view a bigger picture of life. I realized that I'm not the center of the universe. If I'm gone tomorrow, society will continue; there won't be even a blip on the screen of life. Oh, some immediate friends and family would mourn for a while, but soon they too would move forward with their lives.

Each one of us has an impact on the lives we come in contact with on a daily basis. Leadership provides such unique opportunities to impart one's beliefs and philosophies that the responsibility must be taken seriously. It is through leadership that lives are changed. Leadership is about helping others move closer to their potential. Organizations become successful because the people within them are successful. Leaders help make that happen. If we are given the opportunity to lead others, we can do no less than to meet the challenge with a passion for making life a little better for all those we come in contact with. Can you think of a more worthwhile calling in life?

No one can really tell you that you've made the right career choice to be a leader. You have to feel it. You'll know you've made the right choice when the moment arrives for you to step up and provide support for a colleague in pain. In this case I am referring to emotional pain. That's right, emotional pain can be more damaging than any physical pain imaginable, because the body heals but emotions last forever in our minds.

Bonnie was a sixth-grade language arts teacher who displayed a passion for helping her students grow to their potential. The incident that tested her resolve didn't even occur in the classroom but during her after-school bus supervision. It's interesting how circumstances can change lives. The buses were still loading in front of school when a bus driver asked the teacher on duty to assist in removing a disruptive student. Bonnie responded by directing the fourteen-year-old boy to get off the bus. The young man had other ideas. Angry and defiant, he let go with a verbal barrage of profanity and racial assassinations that would have made the east-side gang the 12 Street City Boys proud. After an ugly scene Bonnie convinced the boy to go to the office and call his mother for a ride home.

On that day, Larry was assisting the principal with the usual administrative overload by helping to solve minor discipline problems. Larry was a talented teacher who was looking for some administrative experience as he prepared to enter an administrative credentialing program. A well-respected teacher, Larry confidently stepped in to solve the after-school problem with Bonnie. It was getting uglier by the minute. I had been loading buses at the north side of school and was unaware of the commotion taking place in front of the office. After a few minutes the buses rolled away, and my mind shifted toward a Friday afternoon "happy hour" as another long week came to an end. As I entered the office, Larry came rushing up saying, "I think you better handle this one, it's out of my league."

With a Friday afternoon mind-set, I entered the conference room and found Bonnie and Larry seated at the conference table and an angry mother obviously just waiting to devour the next victim to enter the room. Sensing the tension from whatever discussion had just taken place, I attempted to speak slowly while clearly restating the facts that had been presented by Larry. Mother continued to assume and aggressive position, refusing to sit so as to maintain her psychological advantage over the rest of us in the room. She was loud and aggressive. After listening and evaluating, I informed her that her son would be off the bus for five days and would be suspended from school for using profanity to the teacher on supervision. Trying to focus on issues while stressing the importance for her son's following the directions from any staff member at any time at school, I used the liability angle, emphasizing that we are responsible for his safety and that I was sure she would want us to take actions that would ensure her son's safety in an emergency situation. All students must follow our directions to maintain order and safety, I said. I told her I would meet with her and her son upon his return to school so that we could build a plan for his success.

After Mother took her son and left the school, Bonnie broke down in uncontrollable tears. "Why am I even here? How can people be so cruel and rude?" She kept saying the same phrases, trying to control the tears that were streaming down her face and looking to me for comfort. I wished I had the answers. In situations where colleagues are emotionally wounded, it is the leader's responsibility to give support and help them focus on the big picture. Emotional crisis tends to create a funnel effect—that is, perceptions become clouded by emotions that concentrate as if in the narrow end of a funnel. Try to help a wounded colleague remember there is a wide end of the funnel, by focusing on their positive traits and their contributions to the many lives they impact on a daily basis. In the middle of battle, leaders must keep the dream alive. Two months into the next school year, Bonnie resigned from her teaching position in the district to pursue other interests. We lost a good teacher that day, and I felt helpless.

Whether in education or business, a customer-service mentality is evident in high-performing organizations even when reason is stretched to the limits of decency. The more we study research in the areas of group interaction, the more obvious the human factor becomes. The human factor will not go away. It's out there and always has been. So why do so many organizations fail to seize the common sense of building high-performing organizations around the people within? Is it selfishness, greed, power, ego, incompetence, poor preparation, or just obliviousness? I wish I had the answer. Perhaps too many leaders see the forest before the trees. Think about it: the trees *are* the forest.

If the goal of change is to create something better, then it seems the quest is never ending. Perhaps Henry David Thoreau found the essence of personal satisfaction when he wrestled with his own purpose, writing about his journey to the woods. He went to the woods to confront "only the essential facts of life, and see if I could not learn what it had to teach." There he discovered a desire to grow to the highest level of existence possible. "I wanted to live deep and suck out all the marrow of life, to live so sturdily and Spartan-like as to put to rout all that was not life." When he left the woods, he had come to a conclusion about purpose and desire. "I learned this, at least, by my experiment; that if one advances confidently in the direction of his dreams, and endeavors to live the life which he has imagined, he will meet with success unexpected in common hours" (Fulghum 1997, 47).

5

TURNAROUND

*Winning is a journey rather than a destination. It is found some-
where beyond the land of dreams where harmony reigns. Lurking
between hope and faith, concealed by doubt and arrogance, it is revealed in simplicity. There are no directions or maps, because the
voyage never ends. It is not a place defined by things but rather by
a state of unity where the common cause is greater than any pursuit of individual satisfaction.*

Turnaround is serious business and demands dedicated and caring leaders. Over time I have found that successful leaders have learned how to
avoid the temptations of becoming a dictator or a micromanager by creating
environments where mutual trust and dedication determine the character of
their schools. These leaders have learned how to check their egos at the door
before entering the arena.

The change process actually becomes an evolution of human dynamics
within an organization. We are about to see how positive change requires the
efforts of all who are involved. Success may have to follow failure. Ariyaratine, the founder of the community organization Sarvodaya Shramadana of
Sri Lanka, expresses his views on the dangers of change in this way: "When
we try to bring about change in our societies, we are treated first with indif-
ference, then with ridicule, then with abuse and then with oppression. And
finally, the greatest challenge is thrown at us: We are treated with respect.
This is the most dangerous stage" (Kleiner et al. 1994, 16).

Even with the best of plans, change can bring unpredictable results. My college roommate once told me how he learned about change and timing. Aaron had gone into a drug store to buy condoms. The pharmacist said the condoms came in packs of six or twelve and asked which he wanted. "Well," Aaron said nervously, "I'll take the twelve pack." The pharmacist raised his eyebrows then proceeded to complete the purchase. The plan was in place, for that very evening Aaron had been invited for dinner at his girlfriend's house. It was one of those meet-the-parents events. After introductions, the family moved into the dining room and sat at a beautifully prepared table. Everything was in place for a special evening. Aaron seemed understandably nervous and suddenly asked if he could give the blessing. His girlfriend was surprised and pleased by his attempt to impress her parents. But, after fifteen minutes the family began to squirm as he continued with the longest blessing they had ever heard. Curious, she leaned over and whispered to him, "I didn't know you were so religious." He turned and whispered back to her, "I didn't know your father was the pharmacist."

Accepting the premise that change is inevitable, the question of school improvement becomes one of selecting an appropriate change-implementation model. An investigation of current literature reveals that elements of the change process apply to all types of organizations. Current research describes how leaders have successfully used the change process to transform their organizations. My research of how California Distinguished Schools used change to implement positive new outcomes identified the change efforts of award-winning educational leaders. The results of the study formed a template to be used for implementing educational change.

Improving public education is always a hot topic. From political debates to lunchroom bickering, controversial suggestions abound. Everyone has an opinion. One of the most interesting solutions I have found came from a principal who worked the numbers. Remember that almost anything can be justified on paper. His solution would ease education's budget crisis. The first step would be to redesignate every public school as a prison. He said the kids wouldn't mind, since many feel their mandatory education is more like a sentence than an opportunity anyway. Every child would be given a thirteen-year prison sentence at age five with the possibility of a four-year extension. States currently spend an annual average of $7,000 per student on education, yet the annual average cost per prison inmate is $27,000. Our schools would then be considered critically underfunded institutions and would qualify for additional federal reform funding. What a deal! And you thought public education wasn't creative. Remember, anything is possible on paper.

Now our journey through the change process takes us to the heart of the human factor. Before undertaking any human endeavor, there must be a starting point. But where? Have you ever seen new leaders who were so eager to make a difference that they jumped into the middle of the change process without a clear assessment of current conditions? How can we make changes until we identify what needs to be changed? The classic problem-solving model tells us to analyze current conditions first. Identify areas in need of change, then plan the implementation, and lastly, take action. Through years of observing successful programs in schools and organizations, I have seen how analysis is used to create and sustain effective change. Change efforts follow a logical sequence that when applied in the proper order can improve the chances for successful implementation.

1. Determine the condition of the organization prior to the change.
2. What needs to change?
3. Why should I personally take on the challenge of guiding a change effort?
4. Establish a new vision.
5. Communicate the new vision.
6. Create ownership for the new vision.
7. Develop an action plan.
8. Determine a timeline for implementing the first changes.
9. Evaluate progress toward the new outcome.
10. Identifying resistance to the change effort.
11. Overcome resistance to the change.
12. Build the change effort into the culture of the organization.

Many educators and researchers have focused their attention on the reform efforts of the 1980s in an effort to find successful reform models. Longitudinal data is now clarifying some of the reform efforts of that era. Time will tell if that reform period actually produced meaningful changes or was just another swing of the pendulum. Author and educator Terry Deal of Vanderbilt University has stated, "If history is our guide, the outcome is fairly certain. Very little of any significance in schools will change" (DuFour and Eaker 1992, x). We can learn from any change effort, whether successful or not. We are also learning from the current accountability movement that is sweeping the nation. The human factor will attempt to identify successful change efforts, thereby creating a blueprint for the next swing of the pendulum—because the pendulum never stops.

Across America education is being scrutinized for its product. Can we teach our students to be proud of their name? Signing their names on their work is a sign of ownership signifying they had turned in their best efforts. What will our future hold when the future looks like Edgar's tenth-grade biology report? "The city purifies its water supply by filtering the water and then forcing it through an aviator." I have deep concerns for our pilots if someday Edgar writes a water purification manual.

Many observers actually seek to define the product of education. Freed (1998) studied the ingredients of institutional cultures in *The Challenge of Change: Creating a Quality Culture:* "The public is demanding a clear purpose for existence" (p. 4). It is public knowledge that arguments continue over the direction of educational programs and curriculum. Should a conservative back-to-the-basics approach take precedence over a more liberalized curriculum focusing on social issues? Where does career education fit into the equation of a balanced curriculum? Then there are the needs imposed by the growing diversity of the United States. The U.S. Census Bureau released the 2000 statistics indicating that diversity in America has grown substantially over the last ten years. The bureau data showed that from 1990 to 2000, the country has experienced a 57.9 percent increase in its Hispanic population and a 48.3 percent increase in its Asian population (U.S. Census Bureau 2001). Such growth presents challenges for educators as they plan the most effective instructional methods for language acquisition.

Debate continues among many educators over the variables added to the education equation. The following issues can have a major impact on a school and district: assessment, accountability, teacher preparation, vouchers, charter schools, private and corporate schools, special needs, medications, bilingual versus sheltered or total-immersion programs, technology implementation, school violence, character education, and the role of the government versus local school districts. The list goes on. Some educators believe that more educational opportunities are available today than ever before. Yet for others, the educational institution in America is in chaos. Regardless of the present condition of education, it is generally agreed that the American educational system is influenced by an ever-growing number of social pressures. If chaos exists, the educational system must take the chaos it faces and learn to thrive on it. "The winners of tomorrow will deal proactively with chaos; will look at chaos per se as the source of market advantage, not as a problem" (Peters 1987, xiv).

To some degree, all schools face that exhaustive list of educational concerns. Considering that change in the universe is inevitable, we will focus on the methods educational leaders use to transform their schools into successful organizations.

Covey (1990b), considering the inevitability of change in his book *Principle-Centered Leadership*, states, "The only thing that endures over time is the law of the farm: I must prepare the ground, put in the seed, cultivate it, weed it, water it, then gradually nurture growth and development to full maturity" (p. 17). At first glance such a fundamental analogy seems oversimplified, in light of the complexities of the change process. Upon close examination, however, the literature indicates that common principles of the change process are woven through individual success stories.

Before accepting a change model, an understanding of change itself can clarify the process. Change is more than rearranging the furniture and schedules or replacing signs on office doors. Rather than just implementing change for change's sake, analyze the current condition of an organization to provide data to validate a change effort. Leaders who successfully implement positive changes in their schools have a clear understanding of the guiding principles associated with organizational change. Deming believes that quantum change is possible in developing quality schools. Change reinforces natural inclinations and beliefs (Rhodes 1990, 26). Each educational leader must determine the outcomes of his or her change efforts prior to implementation. Just as Olympic athletes visualize success, educational leaders must also establish a clear vision of their final product. Striving to improve the quality of education is a worthy and justifiable effort. Deming further states that creating quality schools involves three initial steps:

- Developing community understanding
- Establishing local business partnerships
- Managing schools as adult learning systems

According to Deming, it would seem foolish for an educational leader to initiate a change model that is inconsistent with the beliefs of the local community. Likewise, an implementation plan that does not adequately provide teacher training is unlikely to produce systemic change. Therefore, analysis of current conditions should include community beliefs and teacher training while reinforcing business connections to change results from the existing relationships and the possibilities of an existing organization (Rhodes 1990, 26).

A Rand Research Brief detailed elements of the *America 2000 Educational Reform* initiative by providing a new paradigm for education known as "whole school designs." Its research stated that high-quality schools used designs that are driven by their mission and instructional program (Hill 1995, 1).

My research has found that schools committed to change developed their own paradigm. Their change efforts were accepted because they were built out of necessity and developed from within rather than having a change model thrust upon them.

- School vision is developed through collaboration.
- Implementation reinforces vision.
- The entire school is involved in successful reform movements.
- Reform efforts were intense for up to three years then ongoing.
- Professional development is necessary to sustain the change.
- A new level of staff organization emerged from the effort.
- Assessment was broad, ongoing, and linked to the vision.

If the pressures for school improvement are intense at the K–12 level, community colleges may face even greater pressures. In community colleges, the desire for change is affected by trends beyond the classroom. Yee's research of community colleges appears to agree with Deming, indicating that societal needs and expectations become external motivators for change (Yee 1998, 1). Other external motivators affecting community colleges include international competition, educational competition, technological developments, legislative action, and funding. Internally, community college reform efforts are affected by changing academic values, curricular reform, and faculty relations with students. Not only are community colleges experiencing change, they were teaching students how to successfully manage change at a personal level. Like K–12 education, community colleges are stressing life-long learning. With an emphasis on outcome-based learning, community colleges are guiding students from accomplishing disconnected tasks to understanding how to accomplish tasks (Yee 1998, 2).

An assessment of the current condition of an organization would not be complete without data pertaining to the personal relationships of its employees. The work of psychologist Frederick Herzberg and behavioral scientist Abraham Maslow identified internal motivators for elementary and secondary teachers. In 1959, Herzberg identified five factors for determining job satisfaction. He found that achievement, recognition, the work itself, responsibility, and advancement were associated with long-term, positive, job performance (Gawel 1997, 3). On the other hand, he found that employee relationships regarding the physical environment of the organization produced only short-term changes (p. 3).

In researching the works of Herzberg and Maslow, Gawel (1997) found that organizational leaders often fail to ask individuals what they want. Leaders often told employees what was needed instead (p. 4).

In attempting to assess current conditions, leaders could learn from the work of Hill (1995), published in *Reinventing Public Education*. Hill found that change must flow through an entire organization if it is to be effective. Hill states, "Schools found that they could not change in important ways if all the rules and governing bodies above them stayed in place" (p. 1). Hill's work suggests the need for long-term school boards to remain open to data-driven decisions while being sensitive to the current needs of the district.

Examining the budget of a school district can reveal priorities and directions without uttering a word. In *Schools for the 21st Century*, Schlecty reiterates that education is still a people business: "To improve schools, one must invest in people, support people and develop people" (DuFour and Eaker 1992, 10). That statement reflects the growing feeling among administrators that employees are the greatest assets of the district. Schlecty's statement seems especially true in view of the fact that an average of 80 percent of the general budget of a school district is set aside for payroll. A teacher employed in a district for twenty-five years at an average annual salary of $45,000 a year will cost a district $1,125,000, plus benefits.

In California the average elementary school district allocates 81 percent of its budget for salaries and benefits. Unified school districts are slightly higher, at 82 percent. The remaining 18 percent covers operating expenses and instructional materials. No wonder public-education funding is often compared to a senior citizen's fixed income. Many districts are forced to aggressively search for supplemental funding in the form of grants. The formation of educational foundations is growing in popularity. Foundations find that local businesses form corporations designed to contribute funds to school districts in an ongoing effort to subsidize decreasing state allocations. The downside is that some districts become dependent upon foundation contributions and are vulnerable to changes leadership and to economic uncertainties.

In his *Creating the New American School*, Richard DuFour studied the elements of human interactions in the work place: "Effective organizations recognize that their greatest assets are the individuals within them" (DuFour and Eaker 1992, 11). When administrators analyze the current conditions of their schools, they would do well to include employee job satisfaction among the list of potential changes. Boyer (1983) believes that the only way to improve schools is through staff development. Accepting the fact that our employees are key ingredients to effective education, DuFour once again refers to the Ernest Boyer work on staff development: "School improvement is about people improvement" (DuFour and Eaker 1992, 5).

School reform movements are sweeping the country with highly publicized accounts of standards and accountability. School reform is a popular political campaign issue, as evidenced by the 2000 presidential election. In California, the governor and the legislature's supportive position on school reform collapsed when the deficit budget cut deep into education in 2002. What a difference a couple of years can make! Considering the scrutiny that public education is under, all concerned would do well to understand that it is impossible to legislate excellence. All stakeholders must share in the vision and implementation if reform is to be effective. Shared values with a commitment to the organization's goals become the heart and soul of an excellent school. When reviewing a school's current condition, it would be wise for the leader to evaluate the school's character in order to determine the potential for sustainable change.

6

LOOK AND LISTEN

One can either ride the wave of change and benefit or resist the forces of change and be crushed.

—I Ching

Do you know the speed of dark? Is it true that 42.7 percent of all statistics are made up on the spot?

I imagine you can find data for just about anything you want. I've even seen people debate whether the sky was blue or some nebulous hue of various colors. We find data interpreted from the media, politics, business, finance, and education, and sometimes data merely supports what we already knew. If the value of art is in the eyes of the beholder, can the interpretation of data be far behind?

There once was a young deacon in our church who was in the process of training to become a priest. One week the priest informed him he would be out of town and asked if the young man would conduct the service and give the sermon. Trying to reassure him, the priest said that the order of worship had been prepared and he was sure the young man wouldn't have any problem with the service. The following week the priest returned and asked one of the church officers how the service had gone during his absence.

"Well, the service went fine," said the church secretary, who then reluctantly added, "The sermon wasn't very good. It was terrible."

The priest cringed and became concerned. Rather than confront the deacon he tried to be supportive by asking him how the service had gone.

"Oh, I don't think the service went very well," said the sorrowful young man. Then with a confident smile he added, "But the sermon was really good. I used one of yours."

Regardless of how objective we try to be, perception influences interpretation. Do you think data are ever manipulated to support a specific agenda? The challenge for the reformer is to initiate a system that gathers untainted data that accurately reveal a present condition.

For leaders seeking change, analysis can lead to paralysis. Yet taking action without analysis can be disastrous. So where does one start to gather data? What data are needed to make intelligent decisions about your organization? Leaders cannot build a better mousetrap unless they first know what's wrong with the old one.

Change was more than a challenge for Lee Jordan; it was a necessity. Jordan was on a career timeline as a new administrator. He knew that if he could put his signature on a successful change effort, he would be able to jump into the next level of his career. It would be a win-win if he could initiate a positive change in his new district. So he searched for the latest and most innovative efforts in school reform he could find. Finally, he identified what he thought would be the next wave of progressive education and began to design his implementation strategy around it. After talking with teachers and longtime district employees, he learned where the problem areas were. The district seemed to be stranded by the force of inertia, and he was confident his new approach was just what the district needed. As a new assistant superintendent for education services, he knew he would have to convince at least one principal to try his plan. After presenting his plan to the superintendent, he skillfully presented the new idea to the six principals at their weekly administrative meeting.

Schools without Walls was a nontraditional reform effort that would improve teacher creativity, he said. The plan provided a supposedly free learning environment where children could learn at their own pace. He cited research labeling traditional education as stifling and limiting to individual creativity. Being a creative guy, he felt the innovative approach was just what Evergreen Elementary School needed. Although longitudinal studies documenting the success of the effort were still in progress, he could picture the Schools without Walls concept receiving popular approval in his district.

The new approach would allow teachers a greater degree of latitude for developing their instructional delivery systems. There would be no bells or specific classes. Reading, writing, and math would be integrated through thematic units. Teachers would work in teams introducing curriculum through a school-wide theme of nature emphasizing faith in the environment. Homework was a dirty word, and tests were open book.

Evergreen's principal began to work with Jordan to design an implementation plan that would rally teachers and parents around the new direction. Soon teachers were working in teams planning new instructional strategies. Jordan even sent a core group of teachers to visit a model of a School without Walls in Oregon. They came back bubbling with excitement and eager to jump into the plan. They told their colleagues that the teachers they visited were able to freely collaborate on innovative lessons and had total instructional freedom.

Sounds like a win-win for all concerned, doesn't it? It could have been, except that a couple of details were left out. You see, in Jordan's eagerness to make an impression on his new district, he failed to adequately assess the community's values. He thought that a rural community would embrace the natural themes of lessons that actually brought farm animals into the classrooms for illustration and motivational purposes. Being a farming community, people believed in order and self-discipline and that the school's primary responsibility was to teach reading, writing, and math. Oh, music and sports were all right too, but people knew what the school's role was in the community. It wasn't written down, but the community's core values had been passed down through generations. Jordan had brought sweet dessert to a meat-and-potatoes community. Filled with empty calories, his reform effort failed to provide the nourishment needed to sustain their core values.

During the first year of implementation, observers began to see a change. At first they couldn't put their finger on it, but an uneasy feeling continued to grow until it became clear they had a problem. The problem was that they were divided as to the cause of the problem. Some change efforts bring about unanticipated results, and Evergreen was getting what they didn't want. The dark side of the human factor had seeped into the change effort, polluting the original intent.

If you have been around children at all, you probably realize how quick they are to adapt to conditions around them. You know that old saying, "If you give kids an inch, they will take a foot." At Evergreen Elementary, it was more like a yard. Too much freedom can be dangerous. Children actually need clearly defined boundaries and feel more comfortable when they are established. Without firm guidelines and expectations, children are unable to bring closure to circumstances in their world. Evergreen children were suddenly thrust into a freedom they couldn't handle. Teachers were given unchecked freedom, but self-serving motives crept into their good intentions.

Student discipline became an issue in the community. Teachers became defensive as they settled deeper into their newfound freedom. Working in teams, they didn't have the pressure to prepare and deliver individual lessons on a daily basis. In some respects, creativity camouflaged complacency.

The bottom line—Lee Jordan got his change, but it wasn't what he expected. Oh, he lasted an additional year, but the change effort was beginning to crumble from within as he continued to lose respect from the district staff. His clever spin only delayed the inevitable. Through a mutual understanding, Jordan moved on to another district, wiser, we can hope, from his experiences. What had gone wrong?

Perhaps his first error was not adequately *looking* and *listening*. He failed to learn the core values of the community and the nature of the teachers at Evergreen. The thought of educational freedom was appealing to teachers who believed the district had not given them the respect they deserved. Even after convincing Evergreen's principal to accept Schools without Walls, Jordan failed to fully examine the skills of the principal. Neither man had the people or management skills to pull off a radical change in a short period of time. An idea is just an idea unless there is skillful leadership to choreograph individuals into a team. Even skilled leaders can have difficulty adjusting to unanticipated events that surface during change efforts. Over time they might, but in this case Lee Jordan was guilty of trying too much too soon. This story reminds me of the tech phrases "Garbage in, garbage out" and "Half in, nothing out." It pays to do your homework.

In order for the change process to be effective, an accurate analysis of current conditions is essential to reveal areas in need of change. For years educators have used a variety of methods to identify areas of change within their schools. Since schools are educational organizations, they actually become clinics for reform. If the goal of education is to produce educated citizens, true reform must be driven by data that accurately describes existing conditions.

In *The Fifth Discipline,* Charlie Kiefer describes the difficulty of information gathering within an organization. When assessing current conditions it is imperative that investigation strategies uncover true conditions (Kleiner et al. 1994, 437). Too often assessments of existing conditions are prejudiced by the culture of the organization. The change agent needs to sift through a variety of information sources in a search for the true conditions. Assessment of existing conditions should be based on objective data rather than the personal interpretations of middle managers, although interpretations can be insightful, taking account of the source.

I'm sure you will find whatever data you are looking for in your evaluation process.

One technique suggests the creation of an imaginary learning organization. The strategy calls for leaders to imagine what an ideal or quality learning organization would be like, and then list those characteristics. Roberts, Ross, and Kleiner suggest questioning that imaginary, ideal learning organization by asking such questions as (Kleiner et al. 1994, 50):

- What policies, events, or aspects of behavior will bring success?
- How do people behave inside the organization?
- What are the differences between the ideal organization and your current organization?

Such questions help form a vision for success. Norman Vincent Peale (1986), known for his work with positive motivation, wrote that positive thinkers become achievers because they have a clearly defined goal: "They knew precisely what they wanted and they went for that goal" (p. 77).

No college football coach today is more respected than Lou Holtz. In his book *Winning Every Day* (1998), he writes about visualizing the goal. "Every victory is won before the game is played" (p. 1). Such a profound statement suggests the importance of using acquired data about an organization to formulate a vision or goal about reforming the organization. We will look deeper into visualization in the section on vision.

Defining learning organizations depends upon accurate data from all areas of the organization. I've found that although objective, written questionnaires from employees can provide relevant data, a combination of formal surveys and an informal inquiry provides a cross section. Meeting the stakeholders personally and asking for their advice can provide valuable insight, not only about the organization but also about the people being interviewed. Everyone in a school has an opinion; when each member of the organization has a personal opportunity to speak with the new leader, they feel valued. Who are the stakeholders? Everyone in the organization is a stakeholder, from teachers, students, parents, secretaries, cooks, custodians, bus drivers, and district personnel to the members of the community at large. Each individual can provide a unique perspective.

Determining the first steps toward designing a learning organization, Kleiner et al. (1994) suggest the following (p. 53):

- Establish key groups:
  - People wanting improvement
  - People who will be involved first in the improvement
- Bringing the groups together
- Divergent thinking
- Ask probing questions about current conditions
- Suggestions for possibilities
- Obstacles to be overcome
- Clarify suggestions
- Consolidate ideas
- Prioritize
- Convergent thinking or a coming together
- Developing an action plan

Divergent thinking requires patience while establishing an accepted norm for mutual, noncombative dialogue. During the inquiry process, trends become more visible as each participant shares feelings that may have been suppressed for years. Therefore, the sensitivity exhibited by the leader becomes a key element in the inquiry process. Instruments bringing quantitative and qualitative data can provide volumes of information for analysis. Typical efforts might include a questionnaire to gather objective data, whereas a more in-depth approach may include interviews, site visits, and discussion groups. A variety of data is essential to reveal an accurate perspective of the culture of an organization. For example, Freed (1998) found that leadership and institutional culture are connected within an organization. He also found that the culture of the organization is a major factor determining the direction of the organization. He identified four primary patterns within an organization (p. 5):

- Leaders are responsible for developing and creating quality cultures
- Existing cultures block change implementation
- A new culture is a product of continuous quality improvement (CQI)
- Changing the culture is required for long-term change

When considering essential data relating to the current condition of an organization, David McCamus, former chairman and CEO of Xerox Canada, speaks of peripheral vision. He suggests looking at the organization through an imaginary wide-angle lens versus a telephoto lens. Such an approach shows how various factors interrelate within the organization (Kleiner et al. 1994, 87).

Perhaps *The Systems Thinker,* by Daniel Kim, is in agreement with McCamus. Systems thinking considers the interrelatedness of forces within organizations. Guiding a staff through systems thinking can develop a broad picture for the organization while shedding light on the seemingly invisible factors that may effect organizational change (Kleiner et al. 1994, 89).

The concept of market research is moving from business to the educational environment. When the task of acquiring an education is viewed as the product of the educational system, the system considers students and parents as consumers. Therefore, understanding consumer needs becomes the driving force for educational change. Dimun (1998) uses this approach in her work *Educational Marketing: An Essential Tool for Managing Change.* She suggests using market research for gathering pertinent data to bring an "outside in" approach to evaluating current conditions. With so much data available, it can become difficult to see the forest for the trees. It becomes necessary to focus on the essential questions that provide a clear picture of the organization. When customer opinions are included in analysis, the big picture takes on a broad perspective. Consumer needs should be identified first and then applied to marketing strategies for the organization (p. 3).

Skillful leaders have the opportunity to use their experience for gaining in-depth insight into the culture of their organizations. The Herzberg theory of motivators suggests that subjectively gathering data can reveal hidden feelings within the culture of the organization. It is even possible that hidden feelings and innermost desires of employees can be revealed only in personal interviews, since some individuals have difficulty articulating their feelings about their jobs (Gawel 1997, 4). For example, relating the Maslow hierarchy of needs to a set of interview questions could reveal a personal disappointment at being passed over for promotion or at lack of recognition within the organization, or even some deep-seated resentment within the organization.

Gathering data doesn't have to be boring. The investigative process actually allows leaders the opportunity to sense the culture of their organizations as well as uncover little-known idiosyncrasies that become obvious only to an outsider. The skillful leader will identify existing forces within the organization without being crushed by those forces. Remember, when you start asking questions, you are causing others to reflect, and sometimes the process reopens old wounds.

It also stands to reason that if you're going to investigate the strengths and weaknesses of your organization, it should be a thorough effort. I once knew a principal who, after taking over his new school during the summer, wanted to make some changes but was in such a hurry to make something dramatic happen that he gathered the data he wanted to hear. His effort resulted in a partial change that eventually died from a lack of support from teachers, who felt they were not given the opportunity to contribute. Then there was the principal who was comfortable with the system that had been in place for years; he believed in the old adage, "Why fix it if it isn't broken?" He subscribed to the philosophy, "Never put off until tomorrow what you can forget about entirely." You can imagine the level of success of those two efforts.

As eager as change agents can be, they would be wise to be patient. Once you enter the change game, the clock is running and timing will be crucial. Successful change efforts usually require more than one area in need of change; therefore, timing and sequence can be vital to the overall success of the entire change effort. Gather all pertinent data to determine an accurate profile of the organization. Spend time reflecting and planning. Confidentially share your implementation plan with a few employees you trust. Not all aspects of the change plan needs to be revealed at the same time. Timing is everything. Negative employees need to be encouraged and guided so they eventually become contributing partners of the change effort.

Successful school leaders use a variety of sources to determine the condition of their organizations. When surveying award-winning schools in California, I found that general surveys were most popular, followed by standardized test data, and that discussions with stakeholders were most effective. Other data gathering strategies included:

- Personal observations
- Staff meetings
- Surveys of the staff, parents, and students
- Test scores
- Departmental self-studies
- Visiting comparable sites
- Discipline records: for students and teacher referral history
- Informal and formal questioning: "Help me understand"
- Graduation rates
- Grades: from students and teacher tendencies
- Spending the first year gathering data and planning for the second year

If you are going to make the effort to jump into the change process, why not spend the extra effort to collect accurate data? Employees will recognize genuine efforts to improve their organization. The accurate collection of data in the change process requires honesty, objectivity, a variety of collection methods, and perhaps most importantly, the ability to listen rather than tell employees what they need.

Have you ever encountered people who just didn't get it?

The Bulldozer

They can't wait to start their sentence even before you complete your phrase. They are determined to get their two cents in and so dominate the conversation. The bulldozer is a dominator prone to control the conversation by bringing the situation into their personal zone or reference. Bulldozers are not comfortable taking unfamiliar paths.

The Eager Beaver

The beavers are so eager to get to the point that they complete your sentences before you do. Whether subtle or belligerent, they don't realize the lack of respect their behavior displays. Beavers mean well and can will get the job done as long as you can live with their energy and impatience.

The Moaner

Moaners can't get the universe in order. Things just don't fit the way they believe they should, so they moan and complain. Moaners will naturally seek their own kind for group moaning sessions that brings the satisfaction of numbers. I must be right because I'm not the only one who feels this way.

The Butterfly

They're out there flitting from one thing to another, never stopping long in any situation. Butterflies are pleasant and can be helpful in a limited way, although they are not widely respected within the kingdom.

The Stinger

Watch out for stingers. Like the worker bees, stingers are busy with tasks and mean well. They often complete their work with efficiency, if everything goes according to plan. Unfortunately, life is not predictable, and when frustrated, stingers get nasty. Once frustrated, they may not take on tasks in the future.

The Sniper

What a guy! At first impression snipers look like the real deal. They usually are efficient, task oriented, and willing to take on major roles in the organization. Snipers, however, have their own agenda. Whether seeking upward mobility or self-gratification, they take secret potshots at the organization. Each shot casts a ray of doubt as they go their way, picking off elements of the organization that don't fit their style.

The Bear

Bears are cute, cuddly, warm, and fuzzy. They can demonstrate strength yet prefer to sit back and just take in the situation from a distance. Bears act when they need to, and when they are ready, they rest; they like to give the farm away to anyone who will perform their tasks. Bears give up control so they won't be bothered with details. Bulldozers and snipers like working for bears.

If you have decided to take on a change effort within your organization, you are to be congratulated for wanting to make a difference. Before you step into the arena, though, it would serve you well to remember why we have two ears but only one mouth.

7

WHAT NEEDS
TO CHANGE?

*The illiterate of the 21st century will not be those who cannot read
and write, but those who cannot learn, unlearn, and relearn.*

—Alvin Toffler

Sometimes change efforts bring surprises. Sometimes any change at all is
a surprise. How often do schools use the same formula just to get from
September to June? I'm sure you would agree that our schools should be
proud of their product. Is the American educational system producing educated children who are emotionally and physically prepared to be productive
citizens?

Actually, the road to quality education is always under construction. But
often the efforts of schools are redundant and lifeless as educators just try to
get through another day. There is nothing wrong practicing to be perfect. After all, we refer to doctors and lawyers as professionals establishing their
practices.

Does our educational system produce robotic and redundant thinkers?
Recently I saw instructions on products that made me question the educational background of marketing professionals. On a bag of chips: *You could
be a winner! No purchase necessary. Details inside.* Wait a minute, am I missing something here? Or an airline packet of nuts: *Instructions: Open
packet, eat nuts.* Kind of makes you wonder about the other policies of that
airline. Now I understand that safety is a concern, but what happened to

common sense that stickers like this can be seen on a new hairdryer: *Do not use while sleeping.* Doesn't everyone use their hairdryer while awake? Just so you know that American education is not alone in producing such enlightenment, a Swedish chainsaw manufacturer stuck this warning label on its product: *Do not attempt to stop chain with your hands or genitals.* Now I'm really worried about what's going on out there.

Change is the enemy of redundancy. Examining current conditions within our organizations requires an objective data-collection process. Results can reveal the obvious as well as the unexpected while exposing established practices that have failed to match intentions. Literature indicates that data alone is meaningless until it is analyzed within the context of the organization. School leaders must look at the change process in light of what is best for their individual schools, realizing that what works for one school may not apply to another. While data can be used to describe an existing condition, yet research and practical experience seems to suggest that reforming an educational organization can take place at a variety of levels. Ron Edmond in 1979 identified the following characteristics of effective schools (DuFour and Eaker 1992, 25):

- Safe and orderly
- Clear mission
- Instructional leadership
- High expectations
- High level of time on task
- Continuous monitoring of student progress
- Positive home–school relations

After analysis is complete, the next question to be asked is: Where do we start? What needs to be changed? There is collective agreement that reform starts in the classroom. Meaningful reform pertains to curriculum and instructional strategies. Traub (1999) cites the work of Yale psychologist James Comer, who believes that schools must first attend to the moral, social, and psychological development issues of children (p. 3). Other educators believe that the curriculum is most important and that the direct instruction model will address the essence of education. The concept of direct instruction illustrates that children will learn what they are taught. In his work *Better by Design*, Traub (1999) states that those who believe in the direct instruction model follow accepted cognitive development and learning theory. "Schools fail because they teach badly" (p. 12).

We cannot definitely say that one approach is successful for all children.

Better by Design lists the most prevalent schoolwide reform approaches. Traub summarizes current reform philosophies, citing practical examples in schools across the country. This brief summary may offer approaches that match the needs revealed from your data collection. Leaders should be free to search out the best applications available to implement their change efforts. Remember, no one approach is right for all schools. By factoring in school demographics, teacher characteristics, facilities, and funding, schools can select parts of several reform philosophies. It would be wise for leaders to allocate funds for leadership teams to visit schools using approaches that may be of interest. Change is something that everyone in the organization will have to live with, so it is imperative that a school does its homework in order to identify solutions that will work for its situation. If improving student achievement is a serious need in your school, your leadership team should study current reform approaches to find the best match for your site. It's like rolling your shopping cart through the supermarket of educational reform.

Accelerated Schools

- A progressive approach for disadvantaged children.
- Setting high expectations rather than a remedial approach.
- Brings in the community for school-based decision making.
- Promotes an open-ended teaching style that is authentic rather than abstract. It is interactive and experiential as well as involving the entire class.
- A variety of teaching methods have a better chance to reach different learning styles.
- Accelerated schools use an interdisciplinary style to master concepts rather than repetition.
- Evidence of positive effects on student achievement is marginal. One study has demonstrated positive effects.

America's Choice

- Academic standards are the core of the reform. There is disagreement as to the standards and whether standards should be imposed by the state or local school districts.
- Develops academic standards in English, math, and science following a hands-on approach known as "applied learning."
- A standardized assessment system is used to measure growth.
- Evidence of positive effects on student achievement is still being conducted, and conclusions are not yet complete.

Coalition of Essential Schools

- Believes that less is more, emphasizes quality and depth of instruction rather than large volumes of material.
- Believes that schools cannot force children to learn in ways that are contrary to their learning styles.
- Student schedules are organized into blocks to promote mastery of the curriculum.
- Students are promoted when they reach a certain level of proficiency.
- Each school has the authority to develop its own curriculum and schedule.
- Students demonstrate proficiency through project-based learning and portfolios.
- Evidence of positive effects on student achievement is mixed. Studies show inconsistent or no effects.

Core Knowledge

- The curriculum is based on content, not process.
- Believes in providing a fact-rich curriculum. Such an approach builds a factual base upon which eventual critical thinking may occur.
- Establishes a curriculum spiral that teaches sequences of facts through each grade level. Students do not repeat the same material in different grades.

- Teachers are free to use a variety of teaching strategies. For example, at some Core Knowledge schools, students learn reading by a combination of whole language and phonics.
- Leadership is required to monitor and guide teachers through the freedom of curricular planning.
- Evidence of positive effects on student achievement is promising.

Direct Instruction

- Believes that breaking down skills into the smallest units help students grasp the assembly line of facts.
- Mastering concepts helps students to understand rules and how facts fit into the big picture. Cognitive skills are broken down into their smallest units for sequential understanding.
- Teachers teach facts and concepts through scripted lessons, wherein students recite answers.
- Phonics used to teach reading. Passing from one level to another takes students from decoding skills to reasoning skills.
- Students are scheduled in homogeneous classes.
- Evidence of positive effects on student achievement is strong. Studies show that the rigorous methodological approach produces positive effects.

Edison Project

- A structure supported by the Edison Company, which contracts with districts and operates charter schools.
- Students are placed in academies, where they stay with their teachers for two to three years. Academies are broken down into "houses" where school culture is emphasized.
- The emphasis is on teaching character and ethics through core values.
- Evidence of positive effects on student achievement is not now available. The Edison Project was first introduced into schools in 1995 in kindergarten through the tenth grade.

Outward Bound

- Emphasizes moral development and the joy of learning through self-discovery.
- Expeditionary learning places students into semester-long interdisciplinary projects. Field trips reinforce concepts taught in the classrooms.
- Evidence of positive effects on student achievement is promising. Three studies show positive effects.

Multiple Intelligences

- Believes that schools should devote as much time to the gifts of music, art, oral presentation, and movement as they do to worksheets, writing, and problem solving.
- "Who you are is more important than what you know."
- Uses multiple pathways of student interest as entry points to the traditional subjects. The interest pathway would lead to a spiral of knowledge within a subject field.
- Evidence of positive effects on student achievement is not now available.

School Development Program

- Emphasizes social, psychological, and moral growth through student-centered teams. Student Study Teams (SSTs) are composed of a parent team, student staff team, and a support team, including psychologist, counselors, and special education teachers.
- Promotes a philosophy of supportive teams to develop children's interpersonal skills.
- James Cormer believes that "Children will not learn unless they are ready to learn."
- Behavior modification is used to reinforce positive behavior.
- School Development Programs transforms school conditions and culture to develop learning readiness.
- Evidence of positive effects on student achievement is promising. Three studies have shown positive effects.

Success for All

- The crisis-intervention program was originally established to benefit inner-city children.
- The K–6 program emphasizes the importance of reading and direct instruction.
- Basic concepts of reading are taught through ninety-minute daily reading sessions. One-on-one tutoring helps students who fall behind the reading sequence.
- Evidence of positive effects on student achievement is strong. Four studies show positive effects (Traub 1999, 4).

With such a variety of applications available, there is no excuse for a school to continue in a nongrowth mode. The selection of an educational approach may be supported or stifled by the prevailing district philosophy. When a staff finds the approach it believes is best for its school, the school leadership should begin the task of educating the district to the benefits of the approach. Often times the district administration and the board of trustees can become an anchor that is stuck firmly in the traditions of the past. If a school's change effort is to be all-inclusive, it is vital that the superintendent be supportive.

Kotter (1996) believes that change takes place when a combination of trust and common goals is shared (p. 65). In his analysis of the business community, he found that building a coalition fosters change. That coalition exists in three phases:

- Finding the right people
- Creating trust
- Developing a common goal

Data analysis may reveal both internal and external areas are in need of change. Political pressures as well as societal needs and expectations represent a few of the external forces influencing change. Once identified, external pressures may affect internal issues within a school. For example, if test scores are an issue for a local community, curricular alignment to standards, teacher training, and hiring credentialed teachers along with instructional strategies become internal issues facing change. Brophy and Good write of the complex factors influencing organizational change: "The research also shows that complex instructional problems cannot be solved with simple prescriptions" (DuFour and Eaker 1992, 11).

A review of meaningful literature can provide valuable insight for school reform efforts. We would be limiting our options if we reviewed only contemporary research on the change process. From a historical perspective, change is the essence of civilization. Over time, rulers come and go, leaving different political landscapes in their wake. It could be said that even in our current volatile political arena, the leaders of tomorrow may discard the decisions made today. Our review of literature on the process of change would be incomplete without investigating the legendary works of the ancients. The *I Ching*, or *Book of Changes*, dating from twelfth-century BC China, is considered one of the oldest books in existence. A combination of wise sayings and religious epigrams, the *I Ching* guided reform efforts of emperors and warriors for thousands of years. In ancient China, the concept of change is one of opposing forces, a concept not widely accepted in Western culture. "Within this idea of change, there is the concept that each individual can either flow with the sway of change and thus personally benefit, or go against the flow and be crushed" (Ho, O'Brien, and Palmer 1986, 50).

At the center of the *I Ching* philosophy are a series of six-line hexagrams, each bearing its own interpretation of events in the universe. Six solid or broken lines make up each hexagram. The lines are matched to wise sayings. The broken lines represent the *yin* forces, and the solid lines represent the *yang*. The ancient Chinese believed that the *yin* and *yang* were the forces that move the universe. The forty-third hexagram, a series of five solid lines and one broken line, is known as the *Kuai,* or the New Outcome. Much of the interpretation of this New Outcome hexagram can be applied to contemporary change models. In their work *The Fortune Teller's I Ching*, Ho, O'Brien, and Palmer (1986) describe the elements of the *Kuai* (p. 147):

- Reestablishing harmony and cooperation begins locally.
- Corrupt leadership is being replaced with wise leadership.
- An honest and virtuous personality is the best weapon for overcoming corrupt authority.
- A generous man shares his knowledge with everyone he meets.

The ancient *Kuai* statement illustrates the parallel between *I Ching* and contemporary change analysis by stating that reestablishing harmony and cooperation begins locally. In *Creating the New American School*, DuFour and Eaker (1992) wrote that the greatest assets of an organization are the individuals within (p. 11).

From ancient wisdom to state-of-the-art decision making, Leonard, Shulman, and Smith (1996), in their work *Application of F-117 Acquisition Strategy to Other Programs in the New Acquisition Environment*, describe how leadership in the Air Force contributed to the success of the highly secret stealth fighter. Four of the Air Force management strategies have conventional applications for organizational change efforts (p. 2):

- Strong and sustained support from leadership
- A willingness to delegate authority to low levels of the organization
- A tolerance for risk taking
- Building a staff of highly qualified people

When determining areas in need of change, leaders may do well to remember a simple motto that came out of the Freed (1998) research, "Preserve the best and improve the rest" (p. 10). He discovered that leaders must be careful not to overlook past success while striving to create a new direction.

Matthews and Karr-Kidwell (1999) describe five factors for broad-based school reform in their work, *The New Technology and Educational Reform* (p. 6):

- Change theory: A complex process that takes up to ten years to fully institutionalize. The theory focuses on changing an organization's structure by considering all aspects of the organization. Matthews describes the work of Schlechty (1990), who argued that relationships, values, and knowledge within the organization need to change before the effort is fully implemented. McAdams (1997) elaborated on the change process: "Structural change requires cultural change"
- Organizational theory: Weick (1992) described the four characteristics of a decentralized decision-making model:
  - Enriching the customer
  - Cooperation to improve competitiveness

- Organization
- Leveraging the impact of people and information.
- State and national politics: Chub and Moe (1991) studied how politics can impede significant school reform because of its inherent tendency to create cumbersome controls and to micromanage.
- Local politics and governance: In 1990, Schlecty wrote that systemic changes require board approval and support. For systemic changes to be implemented. school boards need to maintain the established course in spite of trends and political and community pressures associated with changes in superintendents.
- Leadership theory: Team concepts form the basis of leadership theory as outlined in *The Fifth Discipline* by Senge (Kleiner et al. 1994).

Educational organizations looking to improve the quality of their product may possibly focus on external demands imposed from political and community forces. We have looked at several external forces that may stimulate change; however, deep within an organization beats the heart of sustainable change. The challenge to meaningful change is to create an atmosphere that brings out professional commitment. It stands to reason that school improvement will follow the improvement of the people within. Whether a new state-of-the-art school or a facility overdue for deferred maintenance, school success comes from the people within.

This premise is substantiated by a study by the Rand Corporation (McLaughlin 1990) illustrating the complexity of institutional change: "The best hope of school reform lies in improving schools one building at a time" (DuFour and Eaker 1992, 20).

I found that leaders identified areas that needed to change in their schools prior to being recognized as exemplary schools:

- Clear administrative direction
- Convincing teacher that assessment data are valuable
- Work toward consensus for vision and implementation
- Site administration needed to create a sense of mission
- Open lines of communication
- Create an environment of trust
- Improve leadership

- Replace the site administrator
- Improve the school image in the community
- Need the entire staff to move in the same direction
- Clarify job responsibilities
- Create a schedule that meets students' needs
- Improve campus security
- A new system of positive results in a negative environment
- Leadership from the district level

How does your school match up with that list? If you are like most schools, you could relate to several of those needs. In researching the dynamics of organizational change, I found it interesting that improving classroom instruction accounted for the highest frequency of responses. Improving leadership and communication accounted for 41 percent of the responses. Like most organizations, schools are looking for leadership. Where will the leadership come from? Are leaders born, or can they be developed? All indications show that when individuals possess the right personal skills, leadership strategies can be taught. The challenges our organizations and schools face today create a need for competent leaders equipped with the skills required to initiate meaningful change even under the most difficult situations.

The responsibility for leadership training falls directly on colleges and universities. College and university administrative credentialing programs need to utilize the practical arena of our K–12 schools to blend theory with reality. I've seen Ph.D. candidates who were working as substitute teachers during their graduate training come to our junior high without a clue even how to take attendance, let alone relate to children. Too often college administrative programs overemphasize research and fail to emphasize the human factor. Our schools are not laboratories but learning organizations that must identify with and meet the needs of children. Parents want to believe their schools are dedicated to provide quality education for their children and not facility for experimentation. The stakes are too high to allow a generation to be lost for the sake of radical reform that is inconsistent with the values of a community. If school administrators are to be skillful leaders, they must be more than robotic technicians following a programmed sequence of directions. They must develop a balanced approach to leadership by using objective data along with subjective evaluation while understanding the human factor. Real leaders guide others to reach their potential.

Along with colleges and universities, some administrative organizations have stepped up to offer quality administrative training programs. The Association of California School Administrators provides academies to train new principals. Comprehensive administrative training programs emphasize the human factor. Today, the data-driven accountability movement has become fashionable within educational circles. With such an emphasis on data collection, we must remember that data are merely a collection of information describing circumstances in a given period of time. It takes people to turn cold data into life-changing applications.

So far we have discovered that change is continuous and at the same time inevitable. We have also discovered that the change process is complex and requires skillful leaders who understand the dynamics of human nature. Shall I say it again? Leadership without the human factor is not leadership.

8

VISION

I see things differently and am always willing to look at situations in new and enlivening ways.

—Laurie Beth Jones

Anyone can review current research and discover that vision is the essential element of change. Even the poorest organization is rich with advice. At one time or another, we all conjure up visions of better times. Disgruntled employees who thrive on management assassinations become pseudo-visionaries: *They should never have tried it that way. I could have told them it wouldn't work.* Complainers use instant replays to substantiate their reactive belief in the incompetence of management. Where were the complainers when decisions were being made? There is no risk for those who second-guess, because vision is more than looking back and saying "I told you so." Vision is being proactive by seeing a better way for the future.

But what do we do with a vision once we see the light? Mark Twain (2003) was quick to describe the mind of the visionary: "You cannot depend on your eyes when your imagination is out of focus" (p. 2).

We are about to see that as important as vision is for the growth of an organization, the methods and circumstances used to create the vision determine success or failure. Shared vision builds success. Charlotte Roberts describes the power of a newly energized team; coming to work in a new environment was like "trying to steer seven wild horses instead of beating seven dead horses to move" (Kleiner et al. 1994, 304). Vision is no more than a mental picture of a desired outcome. It takes leadership to translate a vision into reality. Vision is easy to see but most difficult to accomplish. Understanding the human factor can help skilled leaders turn a vision into a positive outcome.

Bo Short's (1997) work *The Foundation of Leadership* emphasizes that the first step to success is visualization. Whether in business or in our personal lives, when we can visualize the results of our goals we gain a brief understanding into the factors impacting those goals. "Whether you are in search of a happy marriage or a successful job, it is imperative that you see this in your mind's eye. Act it out in your mind. You must rehearse your success" (p. 64).

Never underestimate the power of vision. Vision is a personal thing. Like appreciating art, a vision is an image in the mind of the beholder. No two people will view the abstracts of the mind in the same way. The imagination of one of my seventh-grade students illustrated a unique approach to history from his own frame of references and limited research: "During the age of inventions and discoveries, Gutenberg invented removable type and the Bible. Another important invention was the circulation of blood. Sir Walter Raleigh is an historical figure because he invented cigarettes and started smoking. Then there was Sir Francis Drake who circumcised the world with a 100-foot clipper." What's wrong with the big picture here? An eighth-grade girl visualized content in the absence of structure this way: "Queen Elizabeth was the Virgin Queen. As a queen, she was a success. When she exposed herself before her troops, they all cheered."

Dreams are clarified into vision through reflection. The Islamic philosopher Ibn Khaldoun wrote in the *Veritable Nature of Man* that we become aware of that which is outside of our immediate consciousness through our senses. Reflection helps us to understand the order of things (Ulich 1954, 199).

Never be discouraged when your vision is criticized. The world needs dreamers who are constantly seeking new ways to solve old problems. The importance of having a vision goes back thousands of years to the earliest writings of wisdom, such as the book of Proverbs: "Where there is no vision, the people perish" (NIV Topical Study Bible 1989, 304).

How can our organizations seek quality improvement without a plan? They can't, and vision is the road map that clarifies direction. John F. Kennedy is remembered for the vision he imparted to our successful space efforts. He believed that vision is not a one-time thing but an image that is carried and refined by all who share it: "A man may die, nations may rise and fall, but an idea lives on. Ideas have endurance without death" (Short 1997, 65).

The fact that effective leaders have a vision of what they want was a focus of a Pulitzer Prize–winning study of leadership by James McGregor in 1978. McGregor found that a leader must first clarify personal goals before attempting to influence others. He said the demands placed on public schools to solve every social problem result in nothing being done well. Schools that achieve success are able to focus their efforts in specific directions (p. 56).

In their work *Leaders,* Bennis and Nanus (1985) concluded that a powerful vision is the first ingredient in establishing an outstanding organization, that a new vision is viewed as bringing hope for the future of the organization. "If there is a spark of genius in the leadership function at all it must be in this transcending ability, a kind of magic, to assemble, out of the variety of images, signals, forecasts and alternatives, a clearly articulated vision of the future that is at once single, easily understood, clearly desirable, and energizing" (DuFour and Eaker 1992, 23).

Laurie Beth Jones examined the effects of creating a new vision in her book *Jesus CEO: Using Ancient Wisdom for Visionary Leadership* (1995). She writes that Jesus was a turnaround specialist who gave others a new mindset, a turnaround mentality (p. 167). In *Leading Change,* Kotter (1996) states that vision and leadership may be inseparable and that the driving force behind organizational transformation is leadership. Here Kotter describes the characteristics of an effective vision (p. 72):

- Imaginable: presenting a picture of the future
- Desirable: appealing to long-term interests
- Feasible: the goals are realistic
- Focused: narrowing the variables
- Flexible: able to continue with alternative responses
- Communicable: communicates clearly

Vision and mission statements require continuous monitoring to remain on course. Effective leaders establish meaningful dialogue among stakeholders throughout the vision process. For a vision to become a living document, shared decision making and continuous monitoring are essential.

Schools riding the crest of ongoing success seem to display a clear and appealing philosophy. An observer can step foot on the campus of an excellent school and immediately feel the presence of an appealing philosophy. The prevailing philosophy is visible in the way people respond and interact. Such feelings within organizations and schools are not accidental. Careful planning and collective implementation to meet organizational needs become contagious. Establishing a living vision is the result of leadership, consensus, and commitment to sustain the effort. The lifeblood of a vision is the decision-making process used in its development. The DuFour and Eaker (1992) research on excellent schools indicates the factors involved in establishing a shared vision (p. 29):

- Involve the diverse groups within the school.
- Those involved should be respected and influential within the school.
- Maintaining a broad perspective.
- Key policy makers being involved.
- The principal must demonstrate leadership.

How leaders communicate their new vision is almost as important as having a vision at all. Successful school leaders in California said in a survey that they used a personal approach to communicate their vision. I found that one-on-one contact with the staff along with staff meetings was most favorable. Working with leadership teams helped create buy-in for the new vision. Other strategies used to communicate vision include:

- Share the implementation plan with all staff
- Newsletters
- Board presentations
- Parent meetings
- Communicate the mission every day to everyone
- Encourage people to try new things
- Applaud the efforts and achievements of the staff
- Written communication
- Develop buy-in through honest communication
- Establish positive relationships with local newspapers
- Monthly newsletters highlighting the vision and examples of excellence
- Release days for staff development

If vision is the heart of a change process designed to produce systemic reform, reform must be replicable and sustainable after the leader is gone. Paul T. Hill in his work *Reinventing Public Education* (1995) clearly emphasizes the importance of visions that can sustain reform: "The whole idea of school-wide reform is that one can abstract a set of principles, that will make it possible to reproduce the successful practices of good schools" (p. 2).

Alan Scott was a middle-school principal whose reform effort resulted in his school being recognized as a Distinguished School. Before he arrived, it had gone through eight troubled years of revolving-door administrators. Although several positive changes were immediate, the total transformation took five years. A new positive environment encouraged and rewarded individual creativity. The school and the community were proud of their new statewide recognition, and all seemed to be going well. Effective programs were in place, business partnerships had been established, grants had been won, students were involved, the curriculum was aligned to state standards, and the negative forces had been suppressed by a succession of effective innovations. As so often happens with success, the time came when Scott was offered an opportunity to design and build a new school in a large city. For a leader committed to quality education, this was an opportunity that couldn't be passed up. He felt confident that the change efforts he had initiated at the school were on a sound foundation. The staff was strong, and his school would continue to grow in a positive direction with a new principal. Certainly, the new leader would recognize what was in place and continue to nurture growth. All was well in Camelot.

Or was it? Timing is everything.

How deep had the reform effort gone? It had pervaded throughout the school and was recognized by the district—until leadership changed at the top. A new superintendent and a growing self-serving ego on the board lacked the skills to support the innovative environment at the school. The sad story is that the new principal inadvertently began a new systematic change without regard for the delicate balance of innovation and tradition that had made the school a positive learning community. Not wanting to hear about "the way we did it before," the new principal was anxious to create his own programs.

There is a dark side to the human factor. Within the depths of the human spirit lurk ego, ambition, and craving for power. In an effort to exert his authority, the new principal immediately crossed swords with the staff, by meeting each teacher and labeling his or her perceived weaknesses. His first error was to confront his employees with a negative style, immediately challenging them. Where did he get his information? Since he was new to the community, it had to have come from a secondhand point of view. Why didn't he start his administration with a dose of "what's right" rather than "what's wrong," then build changes as he gained the confidence of the staff? You can imagine how his caustic comments went over with the teachers. It was like kids in a tug-of-war. The harder one side pulled, the harder the other side had to pull. If his approach was an attempt to establish a power base, it didn't work. He must not have understood that power is gained by giving. The more we give, the more we get. That is precisely why micromanagers never attain authentic power. They are too busy exerting their will on others and trying to ensure tasks will be performed to their expectations. Such an attitude conveys lack of respect and damages the credibility of the leader.

During the first year, both teachers and parents were frustrated by the principal's insensitive communication and questionable decisions. The school's leadership team tried meeting with the new superintendent but met only token response. Actually, the superintendent, in the process of establishing his own credibility, was not about to act on the advice of what seemed to him a small group of whining teachers. By the end of the year, several of the most effective teachers left, and others retired. Once again, the school was engulfed in change, although this time change was creating a negative environment. The school limped through the first half of the second year with a blind board, a wounded principal, and an ineffective superintendent, until resentment eventually led to the departure of both the principal and the superintendent. Over time board members were replaced by the efforts of an active community.

This ugly scenario is played out time and again throughout the country. Who is to blame? Is it a weak or micromanaging board for not taking decisive action, for failing to hire a candidate with the skills required to become a true leader? Were the roots of the positive changes too shallow? Could the new principal have survived if he had just put his hands in his pockets and rested on the school's laurels? The dynamics of change are fascinating, and everyone involved had an opinion. One thing is certain—change will happen.

I can think of no better example of the impact a leader has on an organization than the dynamic leadership of Tommy Lasorda as manager of the Los Angeles Dodgers. If you are a baseball fan and believe that baseball has played a significant role in shaping American culture, you will understand the magic of 1988. There are profound lessons of leadership we can learn from that season. The ability to hold onto a vision in the midst of criticism can become a decisive decision, as well as a career-shaping decision, for a leader. Whether you are a Dodger fan or not, Lasorda's skills as a crafty manager and motivational leader became legendary. Many so-called experts had said that the 1988 Dodgers didn't belong in the World Series with the great Oakland A's. Regardless of the prevailing opinion, the Dodger leadership had instilled a positive vision that was embraced by the players. There were certainly moments of doubt, as in any organization, but the leader became a cheerleader and knew how to get the most from each player. As we examine the events of the historic 1988 World Series, we discover that the challenges faced by the team leader were not that different from what school leaders face every day. Leadership is about working with people, motivating people, taking risks, and having the faith to delegate, then let go of, authority.

The defining moment for that improbable season came in the bottom of the ninth inning of the first game of the Series. The writers and experts were having a field day comparing the statistics of the two teams. They just knew the Dodgers didn't belong in the Series, let alone have a chance against the A's. The critics felt comfortable with their predications, as mighty Oakland carried a 4-3 lead into the bottom of the ninth inning of that first game. The A's were ready to close the door by bringing in their top reliever, Dennis Eckersley. Now, Eckersley was not just a good relief pitcher, he was widely considered to be the best in baseball. However, the timing was right for those who believed, and Lasorda sent up Kirk Gibson to pinch-hit with a runner on second and two outs.

It had been a career year for Gibson, who would eventually be named the MVP of the league for his no-nonsense approach to the game. He had brought his die-hard attitude to a Dodgers team that subconsciously craved such leadership. However, a grueling season had taken its toll on Gibson, and now he suffered from a severe hamstring injury and could barely walk, let alone swing a bat and run. The ghosts of baseball legend were looking down on Dodger Stadium that night. Baseball history was made when Lasorda sent

Gibson up to pinch-hit in the bottom of the ninth. He limped up to the plate amid the cheers of the crowd. The writers in the press box were already criticizing Lasorda's decision. "Gibson is in obvious pain and will just hurt the team in this crucial situation. What is Lasorda thinking of?"

Such moments are what competitors live for. Tommy Lasorda had a vision for success for that team, and he took a risk. So there was Gibson digging in at the plate, hoping for a little magic. After fouling off several pitches, a one-armed swing sent the next pitch over the right-field wall for a home run to win the game and secure his place in baseball history. Images of Kirk Gibson limping around the bases waving his clenched fist in the air have become a highlight film. Vision, leadership, and timing blended to create momentum that eventually carried the Dodgers to the championship.

I was defining my own leadership skills at that time, and I learned from that incredible finish that ordinary people could perform extraordinary feats. I learned that determination, dedication, and the will to do the very best possible would somehow prevail against the odds. As a leader, Lasorda understood the human factor. He made the right moves, but more importantly, he had instilled a fierce sense of pride that emphasized the concept of the team. Steve Delsohn's stirring work *True Blue* (2001) showed how quick Lasorda was to give credit where it was due: "Whatever credit I got in 1988," he quoted Lasorda as saying, "I owe to those players. Those guys loved each other. They were proud to wear the Dodger uniform. It was a great ball club and a great season" (p. 212).

If vision is the stuff of which dreams are made, the human factor is the recipe that turns dreams into reality. Every organization will have a defining moment, when leaders have an opportunity to step up, to seize the moment, to lead others to their potential. As leaders, our challenge is to lay foundations that will allow us to take advantage of those moments for the benefit of the common cause. If you are in a position of leadership and haven't felt the exhilaration of seeing your team achieve a level of success that is contagious, then it's time to examine whether you have been overwhelmed with the minutiae of the business and to decide whether you will be a leader or a manager.

9

A TIME FOR ACTION

Do not wait for ideal circumstances; they will never come; nor for the best opportunities.

—Janet Erskine Stuart

Alone we can do so little; together we can do so much.

—Helen Keller

Effective leaders learn from every circumstance they face. There is never a point in life when we know it all. Wise leaders keep their minds open to their surrounding environment and tap into the resources of their universe. To those who lead organizations or individuals, life is a laboratory just waiting to be explored and where ideas may surface at any moment. You could be sitting in a 747 as it taxies along the runway. From your seat you look through the window and see a motivational message painted in huge letters inside an open Delta Airlines hangar—"Excellence Is Job One"—and suddenly a new idea flashes in your mind, a new approach to an old situation. It could be a scene from a movie that when applied in your circumstance offers up a new idea. It has been said that doors will open for those who knock. Seek and you will find. Those who look with open minds will find answers.

We have seen how consensus-based decision making can establish a living vision for an organization. The action plan becomes the blueprint for implementing the vision. Examining change efforts between private and public organizations reveals the purpose for the effort. Alcaste Pappas, president of Pappas Consulting, has described the purpose of change. He concludes that private organizations remain focused on profit as their bottom line. On the other hand, public organizations exist to improve society (Dimun 1998, 4).

School leaders who communicate a mission that is focused on improving lives have tapped into the highest levels of human needs. We have seen that Maslow's hierarchy of needs identifies the three highest levels of human experience as having to do with socialization (Gawel 1997, 5):

- Love and belongingness
- Esteem
- Self-actualization

There will be those who label such noble efforts as simply Boy Scout philosophies. Inertia has paralyzed their thinking. Resist their negative attitudes. They can be won over with continuous success stories demonstrating positive examples of changed lives. Keep pounding away with the message that education is a people business and how the efforts of the team fit into the big picture. We in education are not in the tearing-down business. We are in the building-up business. So confidently stand up and tell your staff, parents, students, and community what you believe in. We are against anything that tears down children. That is why in our school there is no sagging or bagging. We are against booze, smokes, dope, and violence. As sure as the rivers flow and the winds blow, we will keep helping people reach their potential. Say it over and over again in as many ways as you can until everyone knows the core values of your organization. Without a common belief, there will be no purpose—and without purpose, inertia wins.

The first step of any journey can be the most difficult. Change requires action, and action requires that first step. Newton's First Law states that a body at rest will remain at rest until an external force is applied. The law of inertia not only pertains to the physical world but is a powerful ingredient in the human factor. Inertia must be overcome for change to take place. Where are we going, and how do we get there?

John Kotter (1996), professor of leadership at the Harvard Business School, lists essential elements of a successful action plan in his book *Leading Change* (p. 21):

- Establish a sense of urgency
- Create a guiding coalition
- Develop a vision and strategy
- Communicate the vision
- Empower others for broad-based action
- Generate short-term wins
- Consolidate gains and produce more chance
- Link new approaches to the culture

If you are building a new vision for your school, think about how you can incorporate these elements in your effort. After gathering data, be sensitive and understanding of what people want and what they need. Remember, there may be a difference between what the staff wants and what the data reveal is needed. Regardless of how subtle your intentions may be, when your new idea hits the fan, it will be evenly distributed. The leader must make the final decision, then carefully orchestrate programs and people into a symphony of success. I still remember how my first principal taught me to lead without others realizing they were being led.

For an action plan to continue to produce desired results under the stress of both internal and external variables, it should be linked to the dynamics of the organization. Bellott and Tutor (1990) researched the dynamics of motivation for teachers through their study *The Tennessee Career Ladder Program, TCLP.* They compared their findings to Herzberg's five motivational factors, which in turn were influenced by Maslow's theory of motivation. Herzberg found that self-actualization became the basis for self-esteem and that self-actualized performance was the basis for reputation. Reputation was defined as the esteem received from others. In contradiction to Herzberg, the TCLP study found that teachers rated salary as the most important reason to participate in the career ladder program. They concluded that self-actualization may have been the highest level on the Maslow hierarchy of needs, but teachers stated that opportunities to increase their salary were prime motivators. The implication for school leaders is that when salary becomes a fixed issue, the next best internal motivator for teachers is esteem (Gawel 1997, 5).

The timeline for implementation of an action plan can be crucial to the initial effectiveness of the entire change effort. Kotter (1996) believes leaders must create a sense of urgency to overcome complacency within the organization. In *Leading Change*, he describes several factors that can lull an organization into a seemingly stable state of mind (p. 5):

- The absence of a major crisis
- Low performance standards
- Too much happy talk from senior management
- Inaccurate roles and responsibilities within the organization
- Inaccurate measurement systems

Kotter disagrees with traditional change theories holding that the first step in the change process is to reform the norms and values of the organization. His current experience reveals that culture cannot be manipulated easily. The most effective changes he has studied indicate that changing culture comes last, not first (p. 21).

The question of whether to implement change immediately or over time has supporters on both sides. The decision must be made in the context of the dynamics of the organization while considering time-sensitive issues that may be involved. From my experience, I agree with Peters (1987), *Thriving on Chaos*, that something must be done immediately in order to demonstrate that the action plan has actually begun. Kotter's (1996) new innovation formula emphasizes that several small application changes should be made as soon as possible (p. 120). A well-planned series of small events can eventually grow into large-scale changes.

Developing a timeline that quickly shows how results can stimulate the entire change effort can provide motivation for further change. Ross Perot, founder of Electronic Data Systems, illustrated the importance of taking action rather than letting analysis paralysis rule the day: "It takes five years to develop a new car in this country. Heck, we won World War II in four years" (Peters 1987, 257).

Excerpts from Cleary's edition (1998) of *Mastering the Art of War*, by the ancient Chinese master Sun Tzu, describe how to establish advantage in battle through a carefully orchestrated timeline. Those who are first in position have the advantage. Those waiting to enter the battle last will be worn out and defeated (p. 103). The ancient master taught that taking the initiative by moving quickly would lead to victory. Cleary describes the wisdom of the ancient work *Extraordinary Strategies of a Hundred Battles* by Liu Ji. Based on *Mastering the Art of War,* it defines the essence of change: "The ability to gain victory by changing and adapting according to opponents is called genius" (p. 71).

In his book *Results: The Key to Continuous School Improvement* (1996), Mike Schmoker (1996) cites evidence from several school studies indicating rapid action can bring rapid results. Of the schools reviewed, Schmoker found the timeline for implementing change varied from four weeks to one year (p. 50). Schmoker's work reinforces the assertion by Kotter that a sense of urgency must be supported with rapid action (Kotter 1996, 21). If Kotter is right that creating a sense of urgency is required to initiate the change process, it seems logical for educators to accept the fact that our educational system does not meet the needs of all of its students. As long as one child is falling behind and fails to become proficient in the basic skills of reading, writing, and mathematics, education must seek ways to improve. The very nature of public education creates a sense of urgency. For reasons ranging from changing demographics to growing language barriers, some say that public education will never reach full proficiency. Others say that trying to bring excellence to public education is like swimming upstream.

I don't know all the answers, but I know that salmon swim upstream against incredible obstacles. World-class athletes overcome pain and suffering to realize their dreams. Corporate organizations overcome resistance on their way to success. Just look at the obstacles our own country overcame just to exist; why can't public education overcome the obstacles in its path? It won't be easy, but it can be done. The end result may not look like our original intention. Leaders should be aware that the success of public education will depend upon the political climate of the time, because without substantial support public education will be doomed to mediocrity and excuses. When leaders find themselves in the midst of chaos, they do well to narrow the focus of their change effort in order to do something well, then build success one step at a time.

Some leaders believe incremental change over time is the more prudent method of implementation. Research indicates that change can be immediate and still be effective over time. Whether incremental or comprehensive, school reform is likely to combine elements from various strategies that are meaningful to the specific school (Traub 1999, 13). In *The New Technology and Educational Reform,* Matthews and Karr-Kidwell (1999, 17) write that technology, by its very nature, is an ideal model for rapid implementation.

Short-term success can be contagious. The staff will recognize genuine effort and will eventually choose to be a part of the movement. Once small victories become obvious, skillful leaders keep the momentum moving forward by giving credit to those responsible and by celebrating success. Like a snowball going downhill, momentum will gain speed when the staff recognizes the link to long-term goals.

Successful school leaders use the entire school community to build ownership for the new vision. How else can ownership develop without total involvement of all concerned? Leaders also built trust by delegating responsibility. As leaders, we must avoid the temptation to micromanage everything in the organization. Believing that we are the only ones who can get the job done right sends a message of a lack of confidence in those to whom we delegate. Give it up and let go, and others will respect you for giving them a chance. You would be wise to monitor progress, but let others make it happen.

Perhaps the best demonstration of fulfilling a vision is for the leader to walk their talk so that everyone will see a living example. Successful leaders do not stow themselves away in their offices only to emerge for public events. Get out amongst 'em and carry the banner for change. Teachers will be more apt to believe when they see the principal rolling up his or her sleeves and personally getting involved in the action plan. Then, sooner or later, someone else will pick up the banner and proudly carry it forward also. At that point, the change process has become internalized, as others will begin to follow.

Involving a diverse group of staff members for decision making will not only bring ownership to the effort but broaden the sources of creative ideas. Don't be afraid of confrontations. Enjoy dissenting dialogue through meaningful debate. Leaders who have built firm foundations will have the strength to withstand the strong winds of criticism. Leaders who take on challenges are more likely to be respected than those who avoid confrontations. Stand firm for the cause you believe in, and you will find the answers when verbal challenges are hurled in your direction.

I found that successful school leaders implemented their action plans in a variety of ways:

- Used data to build a case for the new plan.
- Included the entire school community in the process.
- Built trust by delegating responsibility.
- Used staff development for continued training and problem solving.
- Developed leaders within the staff.
- Continually spoke of high expectations.
- Established benchmarks and reviewed mission progress.
- Encouraged and gave opportunities for staff participation.
- Developed acceptance through patience by presenting a low threat to new ideas.
- Promoted the concept of team first.
- Established committees with a timeline for results.
- Established student groups to address issues.
- The staff felt validated when results supported change efforts.
- The leader continually helped the staff believe "we can get there."
- Helped the staff understand what was in it for them.

Establishing a timeline for implementation helps to organize all aspects of the change effort. In fact, the timeline can make or break a change effort. It has been said that timing is everything, and that is especially true for those attempting to change the culture of an organization. Some leaders believe that something must be changed immediately to capture the spirit of change. When researching Distinguished Schools, I asked educational leaders to describe the changes they implemented over time—from one week to a month for immediate changes and for a month to a year for longer-term changes. Look at the following list and see how many responses required additional funding. Increased funding is not the determining issue for school reform.

Changes that were initiated immediately (one week to one month):

- Led by example
- Visited classrooms daily
- Scheduled students according to their needs
- Shared the process for decision making

- Created an open-door policy
- New discipline policy emphasizing consistent consequences
- Developed a strategic planning process
- Sought immediate input from stakeholders
- Refined the budget process
- Instilled better staff communication: email bulletins, morning staff meeting, release time for team planning
- Set reachable expectations
- Shared information, kept no secrets
- Validated staff as individuals
- Continued to build credibility as a leader

Changes initiated over time (one month to one year):

- Monthly evaluation meetings
- Created families within the core curricular areas of English, mathematics, history, and science
- Sent leadership team to training
- Prepared the staff for changes over time
- Raised awareness while addressing goals
- Established a new organizational structure for the school
- Reduced class sizes
- Aligned the school to academic standards
- Expanded the team concept

In chapter 5, we saw that too much data can lead to a paralysis of analysis. Further, we have seen that if organizational change is to be effective, there must be a carefully orchestrated plan. Unfortunately, that's as far as many schools and organizations get. If the planning time is too long, the ripples of urgency dissolve into the calm waters of the status quo. There comes a time to end the talking and start the walking. Don't be afraid of failure. A carefully planned honest effort will bring something positive to your school, and you will be the better for it. Perhaps over time another change effort will be needed to complete the process.

In *The Autocrat of the Breakfast Table,* published in 1891, Oliver Wendell Holmes wrote about the essence of a meaningful life: "I find the great thing in this world is not so much where we stand, as in what direction we are moving: To reach the port of heaven, we must sail sometimes with the wind and sometimes against it, but we must sail, and not drift, nor lie at anchor" (Platt 1993, 3).

The human factor is all about understanding and applying the principles of human nature in the change process. All too often leaders intellectualize their change efforts. Don't let analysis lead to paralysis. There is, of course, a time to plan and mobilize your troops for the battle of change. But eventually, action must take place, or the troops will lose confidence in their leader. Some of the most effective leaders both large and small were not intellectuals but people who understood people. Lou Holtz and Tommy Lasorda came up through the ranks of their professions, continually refining their skills. They could relate to the feelings of those around them, because they saw the big picture. Some of the best coaches have not been stars but team players who rode the bench. From their vantage point, they could see how the variety of emotions and egos contributed to the team effort.

Are leaders born, or are they made? There is no question that there are charismatic individuals who command respect that others can only strive for. Leadership can be developed when the fundamentals of the human factor are honestly applied to the decision-making process. Creative leaders build opportunities for their teams to achieve continuous success. Remember that complacency is a powerful force. If you want change, make something happen. Too many organizations are like the woman who said, "The only thing I have in common with my husband is that we were married on the same day." Just being there is not enough.

10

RESISTANCE

Never underestimate the magnitude of the forces that reinforce complacency and that help maintain the status quo.

—John Kotter

"Oh, we tried that a couple of years ago, and it didn't work. That won't work with our kids," said the English teacher to the new principal.

Ah, cold water thrown on a warm idea. That classic response has probably been echoed in every organization that ever existed, at one time or another. So, as a leader, what do you do when you step into a situation where the odds are against you? What do you do when organizational prejudice manifests itself through the actions of pervasive negative undercurrents?

Listen, observe, and learn then carefully make your plans before entering the battle. Don't underestimate that metaphor, because if you are attempting to initiate change in the midst of a long-standing culture, there will be a battle. It will not be easy, but if the cause is just, and if people will benefit from the change, hold firm and press on. For principals attempting school reform, the stakes are high. I'm talking about a career here. The success or failure of the change effort will forever mark a principal's résumé. So, chose your battles wisely, then skillfully orchestrate your plan, so you and your organization may experience the exhilaration of victory.

Dissension is natural, and confrontation is inevitable. I remember the comment from a fellow principal as we were leaving a particularly difficult negotiating session: "Darwin was right."

Rarely will two people see things in the same way. If perception is reality, then all is relative. Yet the key to persuasion or negotiation is to understand the other side without emotional prejudice. Our nation was built on dissension. The fact that respectful people can disagree is illustrated by two legends of our democracy. Thomas Jefferson and Alexander Hamilton had differing views on the central government. They discovered the power of the press to carry their views to the public. The bitter differences between the two men created divisions in the new republic as supporters made their allegiances in 1879. It was a time of change and compromise.

The alteration of an existing condition implies that unknown events will take place. Not all change efforts will be successful. Some organizations carry the scars from unsuccessful reform attempts or feel they are the victims of changes that were forced upon them. The results leave painful memories and natural skepticism toward new change efforts. If you are walking into a new situation expecting to make changes, your first step it is to learn the history and become part of the culture before initiating a change of direction. Evidence reveals that organizations that succeed have done so under the direction of skillful leadership. In spite of the pain that may be associated with changing an existing condition, significant change that produces new outcomes is possible.

Wisdom through the ages illustrates the destructive force of internal dissension. The best-laid plans for change can be shattered if an atmosphere of dissension exists within the staff. From the Sun Tzu classic *Mastering the Art of War*, Thomas Cleary (1989) translates wisdom from ancient China on the importance of harmonizing people: "When people are in harmony, they will fight on their own initiative without exhortation" (p. 51). The *I Ching* speaks of dealing with contention, in the Sung hexagram. The lesson is for leaders to remain confident in the face of opposition: "Respectful behavior will bring good fortune." Leaders must be able to tolerate gossip, yet never pursue the issue: "By staying on the course they will be lucky" (Ho et al. 1986, 69). Jesus spoke of the ill effects of dissension, when he said, "Any kingdom divided against itself will be ruined, and a house divided against itself will fail" (NIV Bible, Matthew 12:25).

That theme was never voiced more eloquently under hostile conditions than at the Illinois Republican state convention in Springfield on June 16, 1858. The conditions were tense that day in an atmosphere of division. The speaker was Abraham Lincoln. He spoke of change and the need to overcome dissension within the union: "A house divided against itself cannot stand. I do not expect the house to fall, but I do expect it will cease to be divided." He spoke of commitment and vision. Research regarding the change process makes clear that leaders must also remain committed to their cause while establishing new visions. Lincoln defined in his address the process of analyzing a current condition: "If we could first know where we are, and whither we are tending, we could better judge what to do, and how to do it" (Claremont Institute 2001).

John Kotter (1996) addresses the pitfalls of dissension in his *Leading Change*. He describes two types of individuals to be avoided at all costs when building a guiding coalition: individuals with self-serving egos and those who create mistrust. Individually or collectively, they can kill teamwork. Kotter's work seems especially appropriate for the leader striving to lead the change process. "Personnel problems that can be ignored during easy times can cause serious trouble in a tougher, faster-moving, globalizing economy" (p. 61).

In *Thriving on Chaos,* Peters (1987) found that the timeline for change can actually contribute to the resistance to that change. He found that the single most significant reason why change efforts stalled was the bureaucracy of the organization itself. It could be that in education, as in business, we overorganize. Seventy-five percent of poorly developed projects suffer from delays as the plans travel laboriously between committees, departments, revisions, and approval to implementation. Successful change efforts of major businesses such as 3-M, Hewlett-Packard, and Frito-Lay have resulted in significantly reduced product-development time by merging divisions and forming cooperative teams (Peters 1987, 262).

Examples of successful change efforts reveal that leaders in these instances created an atmosphere of trust and a willingness to take risks. "Sometimes adversity can work in your favor. Instead of feeling sorry for yourself and using it as an excuse, accept the situation and try to make the most of it. That's how a team develops resilience and character" (Krzyzewski 2000, 103). Successful leaders snatch victory from the wake of defeat by winning small victories and building on success. Some organizations are defeated before they even try to make a change. I have seen old paradigms paralyze creative thinking; perhaps you have too.

If you are going to find success as a leader, you cannot tolerate "snipers" in your organization. Snipers will take potshots at you and your efforts, chipping away at your plan. You may never totally stop snipers, but you can weaken their credibility as your change efforts succeed. When the tide of reform begins to turn in your direction, often the snipers will join the team, because they want to be associated with a winner. Now is the time to analyze your competition and create ways to refocus their negative energy. Be creative; change the playing field, since it is difficult to change the players. In business, personnel can be changed more readily than they can in education. The very nature of education promotes dialogue between educators rather than dictatorial edicts from leaders. As a leader, when you build the foundation for a change effort, remember to create a positive working relationship with your teachers association; you will need its support. Regardless of your feelings about unions and associations, their actions can support or block your action plan. Keep articulating the new vision by instilling a sense of urgency within the staff. Without some feeling of urgency, the status quo, old policies, and procedures will hold on.

Identifying the opposition is essential for overcoming resistance. Even though school leaders must display genuine concern for all staff members, they naturally have their favorites. I once heard the great John Wooden speak of the talented players he'd coached over the years. He said he did have favorites, but he treated them all the same. At a business seminar I heard a dynamic CEO take pride in saying he treated all his employees the same—badly. Certain staff members will attract each other, for a variety of reasons. The same holds true for administrators, although "good buddy" relationships are not as deep between labor and management. I really dislike using that comparison, since it sounds like I'm talking about the teamsters rather than professional educators. Regardless of the term, however, there is a natural separation between management and the staff, and some employees believe you should never get too close to the boss. The role of a school administrator can be lonely, while demanding an enormous amount of giving. We are so busy building others up and solving daily problems that we often neglect our own well-being. Associating with positive people can give you a lift. Avoid small thinkers or high-maintenance people for they can narrow your creativity and drain your time and energy.

Just as 3-M and Hewlett-Packard were able to implement successful changes through the formation of cooperative teams, educational leaders may be able to overcome resistance by the concept of divide and conquer. Forming cooperative teams can break up large tasks while naturally creating buy-in for the mission. Leaders searching for reform could benefit from an understanding of the Katzenbach team-performance curve. In their book, *The Wisdom of Teams*, Katzenbach and Smith (1993) analyzed the dynamics of group interaction and described how individuals work collectively (p. 91):

- Working groups: Interaction to share information, making decisions to help each other meet responsibilities. No real common purpose.
- Pseudo-team: Has not focused on collective performance. No interest in shaping a common purpose. Considered to be the weakest of teams.
- Potential team: Trying to improve performance but requires more clarification of the overall purpose. Has not established collective accountability. Frequently used by organizations.
- Real team: Members with complementary skills committed to a common purpose. They hold themselves mutually accountable. The basic unit of performance.
- High-performance teams: Deeply committed to the growth of each of its members. Will outperform all other teams.

One strategy I've found to be successful in overcoming resistance is that of guilt. Now, I'm not referring to guilt as a negative term but rather as a strategy for creating an image of such profound compassion and logic that even the most hard-line skeptic will join the cause. As leaders, we have to believe it and be able to sell it. By identifying student needs and the disadvantages our young people face if they are less than proficient in reading, math, and writing skills, we focus staff attention back to our main purpose. Identify the need, then build your case for change around the need. Make a compelling argument supported by data. Sometimes you have to shake up the troops to get their attention. I remember emphatically telling our teachers at a staff meeting that we had kids there who would fail correspondence school. They would just send in empty envelopes. At the rate our kids were failing we would have to grant excuses for homework for jury duty. We couldn't afford business as usual.

Leaders don't need to create a sense of urgency about making our students competitive in their generation; it already exists. Unless your school is one of the few high-performing schools in the country where all students are achieving well beyond proficiency, you have serious work to do. As educators we owe it to every child in our school to see that they have more than just equal opportunities but actually achieve at levels that will bring them future success.

One look at a tenth-grade history paper gives more than a clue that this student is in trouble in his pursuit of an educated career in the twenty-first century: "The First World War, caused by the assignation of the Arch-Duck by an anahist, ushered in a new error in the anals of human history." Speaking of content, what about this ninth-grade science answer? "By self-pollination, a farmer may get a flock of long-haired sheep."

Yes, there is a sense of urgency, and educators must focus on something other than the status quo. I believe most teachers have a sincere desire to help children and that it is our task as leaders to kindle a spirit that may have been suppressed by complacency. Our business is education, and our job is teaching. As a site administrator my job is to make sure nothing gets in the way of learning. If that means redesigning the school discipline system or the curriculum, I will do it, because if students fail, we all fail. As educators, our charge is to help students be successful. Our students are our customers, and a customer-service school environment welcomes parents. When the school focuses on the customer, decisions become student driven.

A motto used in the Special Olympics has significance for organizations trying to establish unity. In *Jesus CEO: Using Ancient Wisdom for Visionary Leadership,* Laurie Beth Jones (1995) researched leadership strategies while describing the parables Jesus used to build unity. She describes how teamwork can overcome resistance. From the story of the shepherd who searched for the lost sheep to the king who would not start the feast until every place was filled, Jesus taught teamwork. She continues by describing examples of Amish farmers working together to build a barn for a neighbor, or of career women in Boston who find time to mentor unwed mothers, and of Mother Teresa and AIDS volunteers working together for a common purpose. All follow the same motto, "Nobody wins until we all do" (p. 290).

Just talking about being a team player doesn't make you one, any more than standing in a garage makes you a car. We must carefully plan changes based on the needs of children and teachers. Don't be too proud to learn from your mistakes. Trust me, you can't live long enough to make them all yourself. I've tried!

Mastering the Art of War speaks of the importance of identifying your enemy before planning an attack. Resistors may not be your enemies, but they can definitely hinder your change efforts. I found that complainers actually are seeking a feeling of worth and importance. Sarah was in my office at least twice a day with a variety of complaints. Her attitude had so alienated the staff that she had lost credibility. If you are faced with such a vocal staff member, be careful how you change their situation. Don't crush them, even if the staff would welcome such a put-down. Remember the natural separation of management and labor and that your staff can turn on you in an instant. Initiate change based on need through compassion and integrity, and the staff will recognize genuine leadership.

Tenured to the max, Sarah felt she was untouchable and had occupied a self-appointed watchdog position for the staff. Sarah was given innovative responsibilities, establishing new working teams, that required collaboration to reach consensus. It was a first step along a path of renewed respect for a teacher who meant well but lacked the skills to dissent with dignity.

In *The Fifth Discipline,* Charlotte Roberts found that dissolving barriers was about sharing authority. She found that promoting a new model of relationships required leaders to (Kleiner et al. 1994, 73):

- Share relevant information. Senior management must be the first to open up.
- Share credit through collaboration.
- Reward and recognize. Leaders must recognize and reward honesty and openness.
- Meaningful dialogue. Fostering the freedom and safety for members to talk about relationships and concerns.

Skillful leaders can eliminate or reduce resistance by anticipating the barriers that may arise within their organization. The fundamentals of change follow what I call the "Three Critter Model."

The Herd

The herd has roamed together for years and acts in a particular way. Their pattern has worked before and will continue in the future. From time to time, though, the herd complains about existing conditions. It's too far to the water hole, and there's not enough water when we get there. The old ones just slow us down. We really could use greener grass. But for all their fragmented wisdom, the herd doesn't have the courage or support to step up and start a change effort, because the mustangs control the front, sides, and back of the herd.

The Mustangs

Mustangs are an independent lot who control the movement of the herd and must be convinced that a change is needed before moving in a different direction. Why would those who are in control be willing to change directions? Because they have a sense of responsibility and understand that their power depends on the success of the herd. They will take the herd upstream where there is more water and greener grass, as long as it is safe and will benefit the herd.

The Stallion

There is no question who the leader is here. Either by force or through cunning, the stallion leads the way to safety and plenty. He remains the leader because he is successful, but as soon as his decisions cause trouble for the herd, he will be challenged by the mustangs. If the stallion makes a change, it had better be in the best interest of the herd.

Persistence and visibility help to overcome resistance. Visions that are not openly promoted can easily be forgotten or substituted as the daily routines of the business replace agendas with new urgencies. Keep the change effort alive by walking the walk. Try motivational banners. Set up "post-it" boards where staff members respond to predetermined tasks by posting suggestions for improvement. Slogans and metaphors become visible reminders of a task that involves everyone. The stallion sets the tone. Now, I don't refer to stallions here as militaristic studs dictating a new direction but rather as leaders gaining new respect every day because people see they are not afraid to roll up their sleeves and get in the trenches to get the job done. Leading from within can build a new sense of leadership within your organization, as well as narrow the gap between management and labor.

Resistance to change efforts need not be disheartening. Actually, resistance can become the force that strengthens and solidifies a change effort. There are lessons to be learned from all change efforts. Experience helps. Experience allows us to recognize our mistakes as we make them again. Just as in progressive weight training, the goal of fitness cannot be attained without overcoming resistance. When surveying educational leaders I have found that teachers present the greatest resistance to change. Teachers who are entrenched in their own ways of conducting business tend to recognize that change needs to come from another direction. Many teachers who have developed personal styles and curriculum bases feel comfortable where they are. Perhaps fear of the unknown feeds their reluctance to embrace a new direction. If a leader can recognize such symptoms, strategies can be developed to bring resistors along within the new direction rather than force an issue that may lead to further resistance. For many teachers, their day to celebrate change is the day the leader is booted out or moves on. Then they finally join a team, the team of dissension. Could it be that such a narrow view fails to look at the entire organization? It is the leader's responsibility to keep the global vision paramount in the minds of everyone within the organization. A leader must be relentless in providing opportunities if people within the organization are to recognize that the good of the cause is greater than self-satisfaction. The skillful leader learns the strengths and weaknesses of each individual in order to develop strategies that will begin to chip away at an old system. That's easy to say, much harder to do.

Don Stewart determined that meaningful electives were needed within his middle school. He was starting his first year as principal in a school that had gone through five principals in eight years. He soon found that Boulder Middle School needed more than new electives to change a history of dissension and a poor reputation. Within his first week he was told he too would be carried out on his shield just as other principals had before him. Yet, another insightful leader in the community told him that the school was a diamond in the rough, needing only the right person to polish it to brilliance. Whom was he to believe?

The key factor for Stewart was that he was getting his ducks in line before going into battle. He built a foundation at the district administration level first. Any leader wishing to initiate change must have top-level support. The superintendent was committed to following through with the board's direction to clean up the school. In fact, one morning before the first day of school, Tom, the board president, visited the school and walked into Stewart's office. He was a big, burly man who was committed to improving the small rural community. "I just want you to know that the board is 120 percent behind you, and we will support your actions. Just clean it up."

How often do leaders receive such a commitment from the top? In fact, depending on the situation, some administrators may be skeptical of such commitment, fearing implied pressure to perform or else. Many top-level administrators want change but are reluctant to take the heat or provide the resources needed to implement new directions. But how do you think Don Stewart felt after Tom left his office? Fired up, to say the least, because Stewart understood human nature and could see that Tom was a no-nonsense guy who was interested in results.

So the task of turnaround began. Louise, the lead counselor, in charge of the master schedule, held to the tradition of a predictable schedule that allowed for minimal electives. After all, that's the way they had been doing things for years, and everyone knew who really ran the school. Louise and the old guard felt their students needed the predictability of a traditional schedule that limited free time and kept them on task. They cited the importance of maintaining tight discipline as the reason for their stance. However, the principal soon discovered that their discipline system stressed punitive action and created too many unenforceable rules that really didn't increase proficiency in basic skills. Ironically, discipline problems at the school were perceived to be the main area in need of change. The teachers wanted change but believed it was the students who were at fault. Like water seeking its own level, students are resilient and will respond to whatever situation is placed before them.

In this case, the staff believed they needed to keep tightening down the rules in order to maintain control. However, the issue of school-wide discipline was not about more rules; the real issue was enforcing existing rules through a student-centered philosophy. Just days before the first day of school, Stewart met with student leaders. They told the new principal about the fights and yelling teachers. The campus was beautiful, but walking on the grass was forbidden; it resulted in after-school detention. There was little credibility in detention, because the vice principal was always too busy to monitor detentions, and the kids knew it. Stewart quickly gained a mental picture of a school filled with so many small rules it would be difficult for students even to walk to class without staff members yelling at them. Stewart shifted the focus of the staff toward academic proficiency instead of punitive actions. He announced to the staff and the students that they could now walk on the grass as long as they kept it clean.

It didn't take long for the students to start sitting in small groups at noontime around the trees on the green student quad. The atmosphere was suddenly relaxed, and students felt at ease. At first the teachers were skeptical, but it didn't take long for them to see a more cooperative attitude from the students. Students felt they were given respect and responsibility for keeping the quad clean. This small action was like a single wave that would eventually grow into a tidal wave of success. A new consistent discipline policy was implemented, in which problems were dealt with immediately and teachers became student advocates. Any fool on the street can throw a kid out of a class, but it takes an artist to turnaround a struggling student who has been hammered by the system for years. Oh, there were some students who didn't get the message and didn't fit into the new system. They needed, and got, a change in placement. Twenty-two students were expelled in the first year of the change effort. The board was true to its word and backed Stewart on every expulsion. The atmosphere at the school changed within two weeks. Students felt safe, and teachers enjoyed coming to work every day. Even the snipers had to choose their targets more carefully, because the system was working for everyone's advantage.

It's when people choose to take actions that are mutually beneficial that cooperative relationships are built. Students want to know what's in it for them. Leaders must lead by showing how specific directions will benefit the cause. Teachers must teach students how to be successful within a system that respects the rights of all individuals.

Don Stewart worked each side to bring a new direction to the school, carefully articulating the vision that when students are interested in school, behavior and attendance would improve. This is not rocket science, yet the vision had to be articulated in a way in which there could be no option for anything less than a total commitment to helping students improve. Helping students succeed became the school's core value.

Then there was the Star Class. It had been started a couple of years earlier with good intentions for helping at-risk students, but the philosophy had twisted to meet the personal needs of a couple of teachers. The way it worked was that Mrs. Bornstein and Ms. Tracy selected students who had been identified by the staff as being at-risk. Sounds good so far, doesn't it? They had told the previous principal that because of the rough nature of the students, the two teachers wanted to team-teach and share the class. The dominating personalities of the two teachers persuaded that principal to allow them to tackle this noble challenge, in which they would share a maximum of fifteen students. The program was in its second year when Don Stewart arrived. He found that the two teachers were able to create their own program, pick their own students, make their own rules, because the previous principal had supported their actions rather than face a fight. Stewart soon saw how they had manipulated the weak leadership at the school to their advantage. When one was teaching for the day, the other would leave school to run errands or conduct other personal business. Over time, Mrs. Bornstein had convinced the previous principal that they needed successful students in the class to provide positive role models for the at-risk population. Soon the class roster had fewer and fewer at-risk students and more hand-picked higher-achieving students. What a deal!

The two teachers were strong personalities, and because of the difficulties elsewhere in the troubled school, they had created their own world to meet their own needs. Well, you can imagine what happened when Stewart arrived. He liked the initial concept but soon began inserting truly at-risk students who were in desperate need of intervention. The two teachers suddenly found themselves losing control and balked. They complained and went directly to the superintendent. Now Jack was an experienced superintendent who desperately wanted order restored to the school. He already had information about the true nature of the two teachers but listened intently and said he would get back to them soon. Jack met with Stewart and planned a strategy that would benefit students and build staff morale. After a couple of days, Jack sent a memo to the two teachers decreeing that Don Stewart would examine the Star Class and make recommendations as to its future. Now the bond between the Don Stewart and Jack had been forged at the time of hiring. The two men shared a mutual commitment for helping students, and the superintendent respected the new principal's middle-school experience. Jack understood the human factor. When hiring administrators, he looked for the intangibles. When a candidate said he had to refer to a committee before making a decision, Jack knew he had the wrong man. Have you ever met someone you seem to have known all your life? Perhaps it's that karma thing, or a kindred spirit. Whatever it was, the two men worked together as a team from the moment they met.

After detailed investigation, Stewart met with the two teachers and presented them with a new direction for the Star Class. It called for students to be placed into the program based on existing data and the recommendation of a student study team involving parents and teachers. The opportunities to help needy students would be doubled by creating two classes, so Mrs. Bornstein and Ms. Tracy would each teach her own full-time class. Now the program would meet the needs of more students who really needed an intervention program.

Well, you can imagine the response from the two teachers. They had no place to go with the issue, because suddenly there was no issue. With the backing of the superintendent, Stewart had skillfully communicated the rationale for the new program to the staff. Because the new direction removed difficult students from the mainstream and at the same time provided legitimate interventions designed to help troubled students find success, consensus was established. The decision was based on what was best for the entire staff, not for the benefit of two teachers. The staff was quick to see that the new plan would help more at-risk students by removing difficult students from the mainstream, thereby improving the learning environment. Because it was a student-centered decision, the staff had no option but to agree.

By his action, Stewart demonstrated to the staff that he had vision and clout, and that he would take decisive action for the benefit of students. Because of staff support and the fundamentally sound decision, the two teachers outwardly agreed to the plan. Of course, still being snipers, they attempted to chip away at Stewart behind his back, in any area where they thought they could find a weakness, in order to build a foundation for dissension. Their problem was that Stewart moved fast, implementing a series of successful changes that captured the support of the staff and parents. His credibility was growing faster than the remaining negativists could counter it. The school soon received additional funding from grants requested by carefully selected teams of teachers. Stewart sent teams to conferences, formed academic departments to meet specific curricular needs, and brought into the school a new level of technology of which the teachers hadn't even dreamed. Within the first year, there had been a total turn-around. Stewart counseled Bornstein and Tracy to seek transfers at the end of the school year when they were unable to agree with their new schedules. Have you ever heard of the schedulers from hell? Stewart was then able to hire two new teachers who believed in a student-centered school. It was an-other small victory in the changing of the school culture. The story of Don Stewart really happened, and over time the results led to designation as a Distinguished School. By being persistent and basing decisions on a sound foundation, you can bring positive change to your school too.

Writing in the *Harvard Business Review*, Diane Coutu (2001) argues that few companies truly succeed in implementing meaningful change. Her inves-tigations discovered that most change efforts failed to go deep enough into the heart of the organization, where prevailing culture exists. "Rather, most peo-ple just end up doing the same old things in superficially tweaked ways" (p. 2). Coutu believes that transformational learning is essential to retrain peo-ple to think and perform at more efficient levels. Edgar Schein has been a re-searcher and consultant for Digital, General Foods, Royal Dutch Shell, BP, and a host of other companies. His research on transformational learning can guide leaders in their attempts to retrain their employees. Resistance is usu-ally based on past practice. Schein (1965) believes that an individual's as-sumptions go past the workplace, all the way back to childhood, to the values instilled by parents. If institutional change is desired, then relearning is nec-essary to train employees to think in the corporate way (p. 8).

Sun Tzu wrote that the lesson of strategic assessment has implications for the leader attempting to overcome resistance. The master further suggests that thoroughly understanding your opponent's strengths and weaknesses will lead to victory. When outnumbered, use humility and courtesy, then wait for an opportunity (Cleary 1989, 89). In other words, pick your battles care-fully. Therefore, it can be said that if teachers are the greatest resistance to change, they can also be the greatest supporters of change.

Here are some of the strategies award-winning principals have used to overcome resistance:

- Build a critical mass of supportive staff.
- Personally work with those having problems making changes.
- Give recognition to successful strategies.
- Hold firm until those who resist move on or retire or are counseled out.
- Build on strengths.
- Applaud those who embraced the change.
- Make it clear that "it's time for change."
- Focus on the big picture of quality education for all students.
- Be part of the change or move on.

Dealing with negative people is never pleasant; however, the skillful leader will listen and learn how to change attitudes by removing the dissenter's obstacles. Perhaps the most powerful message a leader can send is by leading by example. Coach Don Shula believed in communicating his work ethic to the Miami Dolphins by example: "I'm no miracle worker. I'm just a guy who rolls up his sleeves and goes to work" (Blanchard and Shula 1995, 86).

Don't be too pleased with yourself when achieving levels of success; even after wholesale victories, there will always be seeds of dissent waiting to sprout. The woods are full of snipers. So be alert and establish a trusted network of the most respected members of your staff. Loyalty will help you navigate through the potholes of dissension. When core values are firmly established, dedicated staff members will counter negative attacks before they ever reach you. They do this because they believe in the cause.

Successful change agents thrive on the competitive nature of the game, the spirit of competition. Leaders experience a euphoric high when their carefully choreographed plans have been skillfully implemented and brought success to entire organizations. So, hold true to the course. Focus on vision and issues, not on personalities, and you too will find that the journey is worth the effort.

III

THE RESULTS
OF CHANGE

11

EVALUATION

The reasonable man adapts himself to the world; the unreasonable one persists in trying to adapt the world to himself.

—George Bernard Shaw

Evaluation of organizational change efforts is not like taking the final exam in English 101. It's not a one-time thing. Evidence indicates that effective leaders do not wait until the end of a process to evaluate its success. We have seen how evaluation of existing conditions provides data that guide the reform process.

We have also seen that successful schools have implemented change through the people within their organizations. Programs, policies, and test scores were not the driving forces behind these successful schools. Research supports the fact that educational leaders recognize the human factor as the essential element of the change process and that evaluation is continuous.

Evaluation measures practice. It is actually very simple. We gather information, analyze data, then make adjustments in the best interests of all concerned. Sometimes information analysis can lead to overly simple decisions, in the absence of rational thought. Consider the teacher in Rochester, New York, who after gathering data made a decision to change a situation. It seems a ten-year-old boy in the class had just uttered very inappropriate sexual reference to another child. Taking an example from times gone by, the teacher took the boy and washed his mouth out with soap, ordering him never to speak that way again. Even when actions seem justified, practice must remain within the confines of the law of the time. In spite of the objections from over forty relatives of children in the class, the teacher was suspended.

Evaluation methods should be carefully constructed to continuously measure the needs of the organization. Leaders need to know what is important, where we are, and where we need to go. From teacher performance evaluations, state standards, student proficiency tests, and mandated reporting, education appears to be overwhelmed with evaluation instruments. Through the entire process leaders are required to build and monitor the culture of their schools.

Edwards Deming believes that performance appraisal is the number-one American management problem (Peters 1987, 597). His appraisal would agree with that of Richard DuFour, who believes that teaching and learning are at the heart of educational reform and that staff development has a direct influence on improvement efforts (DuFour and Eaker 1992, 113).

Measurement results should be continually visible throughout the organization. After data are collected, results should be made accessible to all members of the organization in an easy-to-understand format. States have developed several evaluation processes over the years. The Coordinated Compliance Review (CCR), the Program Quality Review (PQR), the Curriculum Management Audit, and high school accreditation through a WASC study are just a few. In recent years evaluation has moved from watchdog status to self-analysis, to some extent, of school practices. Continuous monitoring by teams of stakeholders creates ownership in the process. One strategy promoted through the PQR process uses charts displayed in the staff room, where teachers can add comments any time during the process. The results are openly visible, and all team members have opportunities to contribute. Such cooperative practice should become the norm for effective communication. The best leadership is visible leadership.

DuFour and Eaker (1992) write that the first step in the improvement process is the assessment of current conditions. *Creating the New American School* provides an overview of effective assessments (p. 41):

- Faculty and parent perception surveys
- Interviews

- Observations
- Examples of student work

Evaluation is actually a dynamic process involving measurement over time. With a variety of evaluation models to choose from, I have found evaluation actually falls into two general categories:

- Informal Evaluation:
  - Observations, discussions, peer support, surveys, clinical evaluations
  - Creative methods to assess current conditions
- Formal Evaluation:
  - Mandated proficiency testing, norm reference tests, standards assessments, locally developed tests
  - Performance evaluation of teachers
  - Curriculum management audits
  - Curriculum: attendance, participation in activities, discipline records, portfolios, grades, SAT scores
  - Performance by subgroups
    - Ethnicity
    - Grade
    - Special programs

Organizations that have implemented successful change have been able to measure what is needed to improve their situations. In order to build credibility, every staff member should be involved in the evaluation process. Focusing and sharing evaluation strategies help to develop an accurate picture of issues being evaluated.

We have heard so much about data-driven decisions as the benchmark for accountability that this politically correct trend has forced subjective analysis into the dark corners of popular practice. The fact is that in the educational setting, subjective analysis is far more frequent, and it is more specific when performed by skilled leaders. Just ask yourself how often your school administers mandated standardized tests. Once a year, perhaps? Will those results be the basis for a series of decisions throughout the year? Probably. Yet monthly benchmark evaluations in curricular areas can provide more accurate assessments that can guide decisions throughout the year.

The point here is that if evaluations are going to shape reform efforts, they should be frequent and varied. Any course on statistics or book on evaluation methods can give you a variety of instruments that measure performance. If you don't want to create your own standardized or norm-referenced measuring instruments, there are plenty available on the shelf. The problem for educators is not in finding tests but in organizing data once they are collected. The multiple responsibilities of the site administrator make it an absolute necessity that district-level administrators perform the service of accumulating and categorizing school data into a format that can be readily used by the site.

Principals use subjective evaluation on a daily basis. Two-minute visits into classrooms can provide a realistic picture of the learning environment. This easy-to-use method outweighs the cumbersome and choreographed formal observations required by contracts. We all know that formal evaluations provide scripted lessons wherein teachers should be performing at their best. Most contracts call for one or two evaluations every other year. I would hate to place my investment portfolio into the hands of a consultant who evaluated progress only once or twice a year. Think about it. Can you, as a leader, create a more meaningful system to supplement the required evaluation template?

I have known several skilled leaders who have developed simplified two-minute evaluations to assist them in their decisions. Use this guide to create your own rubric of what you should see when entering a classroom:

- Students on task and engaged in the lesson
- Meaningful and relevant instruction
- Teacher activity, not sitting at a desk every time you enter the room
- Student work displayed in the room
- Motivational posters and banners
- A variety of teaching strategies
- Multisensual instructional strategies
- Grade-level-appropriate activity
- Standards-based lessons
- Lesson plans available on request
- Positive and constructive comments from the teacher
- Helping students with their hands raised
- A clearly defined classroom routine

- Student desks arranged to allow for group and individual work and easy teacher access

With all the data being thrown at principals, it should be remembered that the heart of the educational process is the activity that takes place between the teacher and the child. We cannot control the condition of the child who enters our school, but we can develop highly trained teachers who know how to teach. It's a simple formula.

If evaluation drives change, change should improve instruction; if instruction is improved, students will improve their levels of proficiency. After all, improved instruction is the essence of schooling. So when you devise a plan to spend staff-development dollars, remember to ask yourself whether teachers will be better off for this effort. Invest wisely.

As evaluation data accumulate, they should be analyzed in relation to the initial purpose for the evaluation. What have we learned?

- Are our students meeting academic standards?
- Are we able to measure what we need to measure, or have variables tainted the results?
- Standardization is essential for objective evaluation.
- Can we demonstrate academic growth over time?
- Can we identify areas in need of interventions?
- Have we discovered new capabilities for our school?
- What is the level of active parent participation with their children's education?

Our review of evaluation has revealed that business as usual is no longer an option for organizations striving to create a quality product. By its very nature, education is about change. We have learned that leadership is essential to guide effective change. In *Legends in Their Own Minds* (1997), Freed seems to have found the key ingredient to the change process: "Without strong leadership from the top, no organizational change has much chance of success" (p. 2).

We have also found that organizations that have successfully implemented change realize that the people within their organizations are the heart of the change process. Even when an organization receives external directives to implement change, the people within the organization have to make the change become reality. Where profit is the bottom line for business, developing people is the bottom line for educational leaders. Learning the difference between leading and managing requires an understanding of human nature.

The change process is complex yet consists of fundamental principles that are consistent with successful change efforts in both business and education. The basic elements of change include but are not limited to strong leadership, an understanding of the personnel involved, analysis of existing conditions, an accepted vision, and an action plan based on needs assessment, shared decision making, open communication, continuous evaluation, and recognition of successful accomplishments. Evidence points to the fact that no single method for implementing change will be effective for all organizations, just as no single method of evaluation should control intelligent decisions.

The integrity of the change effort will have a major impact on its success. The leader must have the ability sell the vision then guide people through the process. Never sacrifice integrity for expedience. I've found that leaders who have been successful over the long haul have been able to blend objective analysis with compassionate leadership.

In *The Fifth Discipline* (Kleiner et al. 1994), Senge uses the work of A. T. Ariyaratine to describe the rollercoaster of emotions that leaders undergo during the change process. It's easier to start initiatives than to bring enduring change. The early stages of the change process are filled with excitement; then progress begins to develop opposition. Once opposition surfaces, the organization begins to feel the overwhelming tug of a desire to preserve the status quo. As success is accepted, change is met with respect; it is then that the process enters the most dangerous stage (p. 16).

Even though education is about change and evaluating change, too much change can bring staff apathy. Follow your plan and carefully implement change for the right reasons, then validate your effort and be done with it. Of course, continuous refinements have to be made, but a teaching staff cannot undergo major reform on a continuous basis. If the change has been done right, move on to the next challenge and build on your success.

We should remember that data accumulated from evaluation are just that, data. Like clay, they become useful only when molded by skilled hands. In evaluating data to guide decisions, leaders must have open minds and be willing to take decisive action. Ronald Reagan summarized his belief in cutting through the paralyzing effects of bureaucracy when he said, "When I've heard all I need to make a decision, I don't take a vote, I make a decision" (Crouch 1995, 98).

12

THE BOTTOM LINE

Success is the result of perfection, hard work, learning from failure, loyalty, and persistence.

—Colin Powell

Successful schools narrow their emphasis to specific goals rather than try to solve all social ills.

—Richard DuFour

The commitment is made, the data are collected, the needs are identified, and the vision is established. How can you put it all together? I hope *The Human Factor in Change* is more than just another "how to" book that takes its place on the bookshelves of obscurity. It could be argued that like so many others, this book contains facts and scenarios that would be helpful in guiding organizations through successful change. The challenge for leaders is to develop a plan for change before the inevitability of unplanned changes takes hold of their organization. Publications containing constructive templates should be free of dust. They should be used in the ongoing quest for positive change. So let us look at the bottom line and some final thoughts on how we can implement positive changes in our organizations.

Of the many elements within the change process we have examined, three in particular stand out:

- Leadership is required to guide desired change.
- Attitudes affect outcomes.
- Change will happen.

The role of leadership is crucial for guiding successful change efforts. Leaders display a desire to dream of a better way. Among his many talents, Ben Franklin was a dreamer who was willing to take risks. In fact, the fifty-six men who signed the Declaration of Independence believed in their dream for independence so much that they were willing to risk their lives by signing the document. Even Franklin's astute writings of his time spoke of the sadness of those who fail to dream: "Most men die from the neck up at age 25 because they stop dreaming" (Crouch 1995, 80).

Are dreamers and visionaries synonymous? You will have to judge for yourself, but remember that mighty oaks grow from small acorns. Walt Disney recognized that dreams can have small beginnings; he once described his entertainment empire by saying, "If you can dream it, you can do it. This whole thing was started by a mouse" (Crouch 1995, 74).

The leadership profile designed by the Hagberg Consulting Group (2001) revealed that the top 16 percent of executives utilize characteristics that recognize the importance of human interaction (p. 1):

- Visionary evangelists
- Consensus and team builders
- Managers of execution
- Knew how to budget their time and effort

Conversely, there once was a school administrator who lived by the seat of his pants. You've probably known such a person who had good intentions but just couldn't get organized enough to stay ahead of the wave. Unsure at best, he had a different view of leadership:

- When in authority, flaunt the power.
- When in trouble, refer to "I told you so."
- When in doubt, follow public opinion.

Such a pattern of decision making lacks humility, respect, and conviction. Did I say decision making? When we asked California school leaders to describe how they implemented change in their schools, we found that they met the responsibility for guiding change efforts by taking a personal approach. They must have done something right to earn statewide recognition as Distinguished Schools. Leaders who were personally involved in the change process sought firsthand data pertaining to the current condition of their schools.

Once initial data were collected and analyzed, we found that 41 percent indicated the importance of leadership and communication required to implement positive changes. I must stop right here, because sometimes such statements seem obvious; it is almost embarrassing to recite such common knowledge. Of course communication is essential for implementing change. Good communication is essential to survive in life, let alone in our careers. So why are so many organizations guilty of that classic line from Paul Newman's movie *Cool Hand Luke*—"What we have here is a failure to communicate"?

The power of communication can change the destiny of a nation. Elections are won or lost because candidates fail to communicate their vision and issues. Why are so many of our organizations floundering financially, professionally, and most of all, ethically? Does Enron sound familiar, or insider trading? Are organizations today suffering from a breakdown in the human factor? Has the greed of capitalism or the personal lust for power overshadowed the core value of integrity? As provocative as those topics are, here we can only speak about what we know best—the business of education.

As with any organization, education has distractions that get in the way of reform. There are times when the minutiae of this business cloud our logical thinking, when we are too busy surviving to do things the right way. When I think about it, doesn't it appear that education is always in a state of change? Throughout my career in education, there has always been a reform movement taking place somewhere. If the old saying that practice makes perfect holds true, then education should be approaching perfection. We keep trying to get it right; if we fail, it is certainly not for lack of desire. The issue of educational reform in America today is a complex one that must be dealt with one classroom at a time. So what have we learned by studying change and the human factor?

- Each situation is unique.
- One answer does not necessarily fit all.
- There are elements derived from best practices that can be used as a guideline for improvement.
- Objective analysis of current conditions provides a starting point for the change process.
- Look before you leap.

GUIDANCE FOR CHANGE

Here is a quick reference that I hope will provide you with valuable insight into the never-ending process of change leading to improved conditions.

Are the Motives for Change Genuine?

There are many good people with good intentions in our schools today. Unfortunately, good intentions last only as long as we remain consciously committed to them. As soon as our focus is distracted, our intentions are compromised. Perhaps they are not totally abandoned, but over time each little distraction chips away at our good intentions, leaving us to wonder what it was we intended to do in the first place. In education, principals and teachers come and go, often leaving a lack of continuity for those who follow. When new leaders face impending deadlines, it's easier to take a plan off the shelf than to initiate a change that follows the interactive template we have discussed. In the long run, business as usual grinds out the same product in the same way. Are schools providing instruction that is compatible with the way the brain learns? The study of human interaction is not an exact science, because of the unlimited variables that are innate to human beings. But when new research becomes available that sheds light on the chemistry of human performance and learning, administrators should make every effort to provide training on it for their teachers.

Sometimes We Are Successful, and Sometimes We Fail

After all, if it worked once, why not give it a try again? I have met only a few leaders who were not committed to their students first and foremost, so I will not be discussing the selfish motives of those who become administrators for personal gain. For those of us who mean well and want to do the best we can but find the trauma of the day-to-day grind in the arena suffocating, there is hope. We know there is only so much a person can do when physically and emotionally exhausted at the end of a day. Concentrate on that thought for a moment while thinking of your staff meetings. Why does the tradition of after-school staff meetings continue to be tolerated? Think about it, do your tired teachers sit in the same seats, week after week, grading papers and giving only token attention to information that could have been distributed through e-mail?

Leaders, take a look at this scene. Is this your best communication effort? At your next staff meeting, try rearranging the furniture. Change the seating arrangement, break up the pattern, then watch the attention level of your staff. Rearrange schedules so the staff meets one hour before school, when minds are fresh. Provide morning munchies along with stimulating and motivating meetings, then watch your staff grow. What about communicating your message with the help of music, video, or other multisensory delivery styles? Take charge and lead, then step back and watch your staff embrace something new, something that works and that is fun.

Ask Questions to Find New Answers

Think about schedules and instruction, and ask yourself how heterogeneous classes meet individual student needs in multi-ability classrooms? Are we doing justice to the gifted and to those in need of remediation? What about the varying skill levels within the class? I've heard it said that we must teach to the middle, that the brighter students can help those who are struggling. Excuse me, but that philosophy doesn't make sense. The last time I checked, children were in school to learn, and teachers were supposed to teach. Who is going to teach those gifted kids who are busy helping other students? Bright children have the right to an enriched curriculum that stimulates their thinking just as much as children who are in need of remedial instruction have a right to specially trained teachers. How can we justify having children assume such a responsibility? There are certainly times for cross-age tutoring, but only in a supplemental role. Looking at education in a time warp reveals that the one-size-fits-all philosophy still prevails. How is teaching to the middle advantageous to all? Flexibility and creativity is needed to provide enriching instruction for all segments of the learning community. Whether for special education, English language development, economically disadvantaged students, or the gifted, specialized training is needed for teachers.

Change Is Difficult

Life is difficult, and no one said our journey on this planet would be easy. However, it can and should be rewarding. Hang onto your vision. Remain focused. Keep the big picture in front of you at all times, because what you do as an ethical educator is a noble calling—and it is right. As an administrator, every day you are changing someone's life forever. The thrill of the hunt is greater than the catch; enjoy the process, and you will also enjoy the results.

We know that leaders have enormous responsibilities to set the tone for others. Too often the personal well-being of the leader is overlooked. Leaders are not superhuman; they struggle through life just as teachers do. Remember, administrators were once teachers too. Keep the mental edge by stepping out of the arena. Find healthy diversions, and most of all, remember your family comes first.

I'm often guilty of not practicing what I preach when it comes to balancing life. As we travel through our careers, take time to understand the purpose of your quest. Regardless of whether you are driven or called, there is more to life than our business. Some administrators stay in the business too long before retiring. State retirement statistics reveal that those who retire at sixty-five draw benefits for a shorter time than those who retire at sixty or before. Life insurance statistics also validate the fact that the longer you work, the shorter your life expectancy. What good will that extra raise on your pay scale be if you can't enjoy it?

It wasn't long ago that I heard a story that crystallized the image of purpose for me. At our monthly administrators meeting the superintendent opened with a metaphor. Dave had often opened with stories, but his crackling voice told me that this time it was different, especially in light of a year filled with the difficulties of budget deficits and personnel reductions. Now, you science-minded folks may be able to relate to this story.

For our meetings we usually sat around a series of tables joined together to form a large square. Today, on the table in front of the superintendent was a large glass jar, a cup of rocks, a cup of gravel, a cup of sand, and a cup of water. He poured the cup of gravel into the jar and asked if the jar was full. Of course not, we responded. He then added the cup of sand. Was the jar full now? No, we said. Next, he added the cup of large rocks that filled the jar to the brim. Once again he asked, was the jar full? It looked full, we said, knowing we were being set up for something. He proceeded to pour the water into the jar until it overflowed onto the table. We all agreed the jar was more than full. Then Dave reached below the table and set another empty jar on the table along with cups of sand, gravel, rocks, and water. With a trembling voice but remaining on task, Dave said the jar represented our life and how we use our time. Once again he poured the rocks into the jar first, saying they represented the important things in life such as our family and our personal well-being. Put first things first. He then proceeded to pour the gravel into the jar, explaining that the gravel represents our careers, job tasks, and things that needed to be done. Next, he added the sand. We could see the sand filtering down between the rocks and gravel. The sand represented irritations, problems, and difficulties, he said. Finally, he poured the cup of water into the jar. We saw that the jar still had room—the water percolated through the sand, gravel, and rocks. The water represented the unexpected things of life that add pressure to a life already full of things. When filled in the right order, the jar held it all. Then Dave looked up and said, "This story is about how we prioritize our lives, and now I'm going to refill my jar of life, so today I announce I am retiring." Silence overcame the room as we pondered the story and the man. Then after a brief moment, applause broke the silence. It was applause of respect.

Change may be difficult, but the process can also be rewarding. It is invigorating to create new ways of doing old things, so enjoy your moment as a leader.

Tough Times Require Tough Leadership

As the year 2004 began, thirty-four states were facing budget deficits. School districts are inheriting the financial crisis gripping the nation. Wise leadership will be needed for schools to survive these tough times. Survival will depend upon establishing financial plans that will not only cut services but at the same time provide resources to maintain quality education. Can quality education prevail when so much energy is shifted into budgetary survival? If you have been in education for any length of time, you undoubtedly have been required to do more with less. For the leader determined to survive tough times, the challenge will be difficult. A balanced philosophy coupled with patience will be required if one is not only to survive but thrive in tough times. For the alert leader, difficult times can provide leverage to achieve a new sense of unity within the organization. Open communication and shared problem solving can bring people together in a way that is unattainable during good times. The sense of urgency becomes real and strengthens the organization's mission. We cannot let quality education suffer, because it will take years to build it back after the crisis has been overcome. Such a rallying cry can become a powerful motivating force for all committed to the cause.

Walk carefully, though, because tough times can also feed the negative forces within your organization. There are those who thrive on tough times by using budget-cutting decisions to validate their positions. Give them new opportunities to join the team through creative problem solving designed to help the cause rather than spending their time in empty criticism. The skillful leader will seize the moment and accentuate the positive. A cofounder of Intel, Gordon Moore, understood economic trends and their effects on organizations: "Recessions always end, and innovation allows some companies to emerge from them stronger than before" (MSNBC, March 18, 2002).

As inspiring as motivational leaders can be, leadership still requires a personal touch. Will Benson was a principal who considered himself to be a motivator. He was highly regarded by his staff as a leader with vision and compassion. Then the budget deficit hit, and preliminary layoff notices were mailed to four of his newer teachers. He had hand-picked a staff of talented teachers and had been investing in their futures through continuous training. He had a plan for each one of them.

The district had followed the law and precisely organized a massive layoff of forty teachers, reduction of class size having been eliminated. The district had to cut costs in order to survive. Along with the other district administrators, Benson attended meetings describing the layoff process. Personal notification of each teacher would fall on the principals; they were given basic strategies for doing it. Benson planned personal meetings with the teachers in order to give them the bad news. His preparations were accurate and according to the book. Legally, he was on solid ground. But there was something missing. He couldn't get the feeling out of his mind that though he was doing all the right things in the right way, it still seemed wrong. On paper the plan made sense, and the action would benefit the district. However, he was still dealing with real, live people, who, no matter how objectively they received the bad news, would have feelings of rejection, disappointment, and eventually anger. It's tough to be a leader.

Ruth was a teacher who displayed an exceptionally positive attitude. Due to the increasing enrollment at the school, Ruth didn't even have a classroom of her own. She had to move from room to room each period, but she never complained and was always gracious and upbeat. How could he tell her she was being laid off?

Benson's meetings with the four teachers went according to plan. They each received the news with a display of understanding and professionalism, although he knew they were hurting inside. It wasn't until a couple of days later that the human factor struck deep in his consciousness. Ruth called to ask for advice about filing her appeal with an administrative law judge. She was well within her rights to ask for an appeal, and she was going to the district office to submit the appropriate paperwork. The wording of the appeal instructions had confused her, however, so she was calling for understanding, and, she hoped, support. As she continued to describe the process to Benson, her voice started to crack; he could tell she was feeling the pressure. It was when she described language on the form referring to her as the "accused" that she couldn't contain herself any longer. "This makes me feel like I've done something wrong," she said. "I've never been accused in a court of law before." Benson tried to offer what little support he could by saying that the court just uses predetermined terms and that she shouldn't take it personally. But the human factor *is* personal.

Let us never forget that the human factor lives in the hearts of all of us. As leaders, we must choose our words carefully and walk the narrow path between management and human leadership. Regardless of how precisely our decisions meet legal statutes, we must remember that we are leaders of people. In times both good and bad, our efforts are really measured by the heart, by how in the years to come people remember how they were treated in the tough times.

How Do Leaders Survive the
Continuous Demands of Their Professions?

Principals can't survive in their positions by limiting their efforts to a forty-hour work week. Try sixty just to stay even with the volume of work. Then throw in Saturday if you actually want to get ahead. Where does your family fit into your busy schedule? Survival as an administrator requires personal priorities that maintain the integrity of nonnegotiable family times. I have to pause at this point to interject a comment made by my wife as she edited this chapter. Her small note in the margin speaks volumes about being an administrator: "*What* family times?" You know what it's like. At times the loneliness at the top hurts. One of our challenges will always be to sift through our professional friendships, determining who are genuine friends and who are merely aligning themselves to the seat of power. Leaders must set the tone for themselves, because their efforts can make or break relationships without their ever knowing it. It may sound harsh, but no one really cares about our personal problems. When the leader walks on the site, he is on stage; everything he does will be scrutinized. The way the leader walks, talks, and greets people sends a powerful message. Leaders should ask themselves: Do people feel good when I'm around them? Do I bring inspiration to others? Am I known as one who can help people solve their problems? Do my actions demonstrate a genuinely caring nature? If you can answer yes, people will follow you.

It becomes easy to slip into the hypercritical mode when dealing with challenges to our directions: "I expected that from him"; or, "She's always so negative." Don't build yourself up from another person's weakness. When we begin to believe that others are the problem, we should look in the mirror; maybe we will see there the real problem.

Time integrates with change to produce a powerful force that can destroy or build ideas and institutions. When institutions fall, so do their leaders. Time can be our biggest enemy. Be sure to align yourself on the building side of change. The Hagberg Consulting Group studied how the top 16 percent of leaders managed their time. They found that 25 percent of a leader's time was used for managing. Team building accounted for 34 percent, while visionary leadership consumed 41 percent (Hagberg Consulting Group 2001). The lesson for us is not to lose sight of our visionary responsibility. If the leader is not the keeper of the flame, who is?

Where Does the Leader Get Inspiration?

The energy required to lead an organization can leave leaders drained both emotionally and physically. Dedicated leaders, who give their all every day, eventually find their own energy depleted from the pressures of their profession. Leaders need inspiration too—from books, conferences, seminars, observations, and collaboration within the leadership circle. Leaders can gain the strength needed for survival. I believe leaders need more than just professional inspiration. There is wisdom to be gained from the ancient Greek philosophy that promotes a healthy mind, body, and spirit.

Establish a routine that budgets time for physical exercise. The positive effects of exercise have been well documented; it not only provides health benefits but provides stress relief. The release of endorphins in the brain during exercise can regulate stress levels. What about that diet? It appears that there are different eating habits among leaders. The corporate CEO diet may be different than that of the hands-on school administrator. During my years as a vice principal, I had forgotten that a meal could be anything other than a sandwich while disciplining students sitting in front of me. Talk about stress. The demands from student discipline, teacher needs, parental pressures, and district directives, not to mention our innate desire to create excellence—no wonder the job never stops. But you have to. "Garbage in, garbage out." Don't let the pressures of your position force you into a steady fast-food diet filled with donuts, burgers, and fries. You are killing yourself. Stop and prioritize.

The spirit has long been recognized as an essential element of a balanced life. Even Plato wrote, "Neither should we ever attempt to cure the body without curing the soul." In 1975 Dr. Herbert Benson, MD, wrote in the *Faith Factor* how faith works with modern medicine, not only building up but curing ailments. The phenomenon of a healthy spiritual life can help us to deal with the pressures associated with leadership (Peal 1986, 86).

Remember that your family is not only your responsibility but also a great source of strength. Don't neglect what you work for. No success in the world can overcome failure in the home.

For many leaders, satisfaction comes from seeing members of their organization succeed. To paraphrase the motto of the Special Olympics, when our teachers win, we all win.

Can Positive Motivation Produce Greater Results Than Negative Motivation?

Encouragement and support build positive working relationships in the workplace and in the classroom. Are you surprised? Everyone wants to know what's in it for them. Describing strategies for developing personal mastery, Peter Senge speaks of the benefits of encouragement and support: "Why offer that encouragement and support? Because it is increasingly clear that learning does not occur in any enduring fashion unless it is sparked by people's own ardent interest and curiosity" (Kleiner et al. 1994, 193). One thing is certain, positive working conditions can produce creativity and enormous personal buy-in.

How far can a compliment go? The wisdom of Mark Twain has an answer: "I can live for two months on one good compliment."

Clear Administrative Direction While Working toward Consensus Is Essential for Implementing a New Vision

The importance of leadership is further demonstrated by our research revealing that 60 percent of leaders use a personal approach to communicate new visions. When it comes to change, there is an old and ironic habit among human beings of running faster when they have lost their way. Leaders should avoid being caught up in the frenzy of the organization's perceived solutions but hold fast to their own data-driven decisions and provide clear direction. Teachers within the school may think they have a solution, but often their perceptions are infected by their proximity to the problem. An outside view can reveal the deep sources of problems and prescribe new solutions. Once your data identify areas of change, select key staff members to bring them into the change effort. Divide and conquer. An essential component of leadership is the ability to influence and organize understanding among members of the organization.

How Fast Should I Implement Changes?

Change research indicates that the timeline for implementing the first changes has an influence on further changes. Data further substantiates the literature demonstrating that over half of the leaders implemented the first changes within the first six months of their implementation plan. I have found that change over time is effective, but something must be done immediately to bring people on board. Initiating some small yet meaningful change at the beginning of the change process has a contagious effect within the organization. Even the dissenters have to recognize that things are going to be different around here and that you, as the leader, mean business.

It Takes Patient Leadership to Overcome Resistance

It is ironic that most resistance comes from teachers within the affected schools. Could it be that teachers fail to grasp new change efforts because leaders fail to communicate effectively? Isn't it interesting how the past can haunt the present and block the future? Leaders will always face the challenges of overcoming old baggage and negative staff attitudes resulting from failed change efforts of the past. Twenty-eight percent of leaders in one survey indicated they encourage people and give recognition to supportive staff members. Leaders remain committed to the change process even in the face of negative staff responses. My research found that 22 percent of the leaders surveyed ignored complaints and continued to move forward, holding firm in the face of negative challenges. Get over it and move on for the good of the cause.

It Takes Leadership to Guide Change Efforts

Successful change efforts are dependent upon performance. Winning builds winning, and losing builds disappointment. Leaders guide the process and at the same time take the praise or criticism for the effort. Change is sustained when defined outcomes begin to match results. It is a simple formula, really. If school discipline is an issue for you and your school is plagued with fights, then follow the change process outlined in *The Human Factor*. If your plan significantly reduces the number of fights, your results have matched your defined outcomes.

You don't have to be a consultant to realize the key ingredients to successful leadership. Our leaders surveyed identified the essence of leadership:

- Leaders have vision.
- Leaders build collaborative teams.

- Leaders learn how to implement change within culture of the school.
- Leaders know how to manage their time.

It Takes Leadership to Build Momentum through a Series of Victories

In his book *Leading Change* (1996), John Kotter describes how leaders initiate a desire for change within their organizations by creating a sense of urgency. Urgency drives the change process. The timeline for implementation becomes a driving force of a change effort once the organization believes that changes are needed within a given period of time. Skilled leaders can orchestrate a sense of urgency that is forceful yet sensitive to the personalities of those involved in the change effort. Small successes feed the change effort and overcome resistance. Overcoming the inertia of the status quo is the greatest challenge for a leader attempting reform. Once small victories are documented, momentum is established.

What Do Schools Want to Accomplish?

The number-one goal of award-winning schools surveyed was improving classroom instruction, then academic proficiency, and then administrative direction and communication. This is the profit margin of our business. In education, our profit is the success of our students; these schools wanted the right thing. Just think about it. Their primary goals were not self-centered but directed toward their customers.

Develop goals that will benefit children and improve working conditions for the staff. Each of these goals is personal and over time will define the culture of your school. Successful leaders are relentless. They take every opportunity to articulate the vision and support those who are moving forward.

A True Leader Knows How to Lead without Others Realizing They Are Being Led

New visions leading to positive new outcomes don't just spring up from staff room gossip. When the conductor carefully orchestrates new directions within the organization, everyone contributes to the symphony. Leaders tap into their teacher's strengths and interests to guide them to new challenges and accomplishments. Through mentoring and monitoring, teachers' skills will continue to grow until they have developed improved instructional strategies to improve student learning.

Can you teach an old dog new tricks? Absolutely! With the right motivation and support, imagination can lead to innovation. Ken was an eighth-grade science teacher in a school undergoing a positive transformation. He was one of the most respected members of the staff and had developed a tradition of quality teaching that spanned two decades. Retirement was just five years away. The new principal quickly realized the respect Ken enjoyed within the staff, and what an excellent ambassador he could be for innovation. Ken was nudged to reach for something he had always wanted. Actually, part of the principal's change plan included the implementation of a technology system that would become transparent in classroom instruction. In this case, "transparent" refers to integrating technology into instruction rather than treating technology as an add-on. Ken's enthusiasm grew as he received new computers, software, and training that would enable him to teach his students how to use multimedia presentations to enhance their reports and presentations. It was like a dream come true for Ken, who had thought he would retire in the darkness of a classroom void of technology. Ken not only learned new technology but eventually trained other teachers during staff development days. It all started by finding a spark of interest, then feeding a growing flame until others would benefit from the warmth of the fire. Sounds simple and uneventful? Ken's newly acquired motivation was actually the result of the principal efficiently using the complex system of change, motivation, and vision. No, the process isn't simple, but the commitment is, and because of such efforts lives are changed.

The attitudes of the teachers will affect the change efforts in schools. Here is another no-brainer. It is amazing to me that in the real world the obvious is so elusive. Models of success can be copied, but they are truly replicated only when they are integrated into an organization's existing culture. Research confirms that teachers' attitudes toward change have the greatest impact on change efforts. We found that 52 percent of the leaders surveyed indicated that change is a process that involves people rather than policies and programs. If change is to be successful, teachers must buy into the effort. Data also shows that teachers provide the greatest resistance to change. Yet, once a change effort is successful, staff enthusiasm becomes the most re-warding part of the change process. The attitudes of teachers toward change significantly influence outcomes.

How Do I Find the Balance between Managing and Leading?

"Managers are people who do things right and leaders are people who do the right thing" (Peters 1987, 464). Can change be initiated without leadership? The answer is yes, but in a leaderless scenario, will the change be what the group intended? Remember that within spontaneous human interactions that are devoid of leadership, dominant personalities will control the results. Collective decisions are suppressed by dominant voices. Without strong, considerate leadership, the timid will be crushed and the dominator will rule. A leader who understands the personalities within his or her organization can guide each member's strengths toward a common cause. That is leadership.

Every Organization Is Capable of Implementing Positive Change

The magic comes from the people within the organization. They have the power to change within themselves; in most cases they just need the right person to guide them to victory. Warren Bennis and Burt Nanus (1985) have studied how leaders work with the tools they are given when leading change: "Leaders articulate and define what has previously remained implicit or un-said; then they invent images, metaphors, and models that provide a focus for new attention. By so doing, they consolidate or challenge prevailing wisdom. In short and essential factor in leadership is the capacity to influence and organize meaning for the members of the organization" (p. 484). It can safely be said that new attitudes make new outcomes.

CHANGE HAPPENS!

In the twenty-first century, survival will become synonymous with change. Change will no longer be a matter of choice but an inevitable fact, one that must be dealt with. A new global economy will force paradigms to shift along with rapidly changing environments. New modes of communication will transmit information before conclusions are even realized. Interdependence among businesses and nations will become the standard rather than the exception.

In the twenty-first century, improvement will also become synonymous with change. As if caught in an evolutionary time warp, organizations will be forced to change or face extinction. In *Leading* Change, John Kotter (1996) summarized the future: "If environmental volatility continues to increase, as most people now predict, the standard organization of the twentieth century will likely become a dinosaur" (p. 161).

In the twenty-first century, education will finally be considered a credible business. Tradition will blend with innovation to produce excellence. Schools will be twenty-four-hour learning communities where children find learning a joy rather than an accumulation of disconnected tasks. We can be sure that society will continue to scrutinize education, looking for new means of accountability. With continued state and federal investments in education, progress evaluation will remain a political reality, but also a personal desire for all who are involved in education.

Despite its challenges, education has a bright future. Powerful learning is already taking place in many districts as vision and policy blend to form partnerships committed to excellence. Successful schools will continue to emulate models of excellence as improvement becomes contagious. There seems to be no shortage of successful models to choose from. The challenge for schools, then, is to implement successful models within the context of their school culture. *The Human Factor in Change* has attempted to focus on that most powerful ingredient of change, people. We have gathered data from current literature and successful schools in an attempt to create a template that may help others improve the quality of education in their schools. Education in itself is a noble quest, and the improvement of education is no longer an option—it is a requirement.

It has been said that there is nothing new under the sun, that life merely extends past experience through one new situation after another. It has also been said that there is a time for everything and that all things will pass. In the present study we have seen that change is inevitable and that human history has documented the challenges of change. According to Deming, quantum change is not only possible but probable in any organization. He believes that within any organization there are natural inclinations to find more effective ways to exist (Rhodes 1990, 2).

The very nature of education is about change. Education in itself is really very simple. In its basic form, education changes human behavior. What goes on between a teacher and a student is an interaction so powerful that lives are changed forever. The inherent desire to improve, whether individually or collectively, drives teachers to improve their skills. Yet in many respects, contemporary educational systems have become their own worst enemies. From increased legislation, unmotivated learners, and disconnected parents to an overregulated bureaucracy, education knee-jerks to each swing of the political pendulum; yet somehow, learning environments remain the same. Has the product of education become so cumbersome that results must be measured by formulas rather than the simplicity of individual achievement?

Somewhere within that burdensome system, educational leaders continue to search for better ways to change lives. Some are successful, and others keep trying. In spite of growing legislation, entitlements, and mandates, some schools emerge as beacons of quality. *The Human Factor in Change* has provided examples drawn from successful schools, examples that should be viewed in relation to your particular situation. Good schools are not perfect, but they have demonstrated that quality education is attainable.

The bottom line of the human factor is about building relationships that eventually lead to optimum human performance. Let's leave the finite sciences to those who love cellular and molecular bioinformatics and the like. The human factor can be seen when common sense is coupled with a passion for developing individual potential to shape the destiny of our society. Far-fetched, trite? I don't think so. I encourage you to ignite the passion within yourself to make life better for all who come in contact with you. Then your bottom line becomes obvious, your conscience is clear, you can sleep at night, and people are better off because of what you do.

13

A TEMPLATE
FOR CHANGE

There is always a better way.

—Thomas Edison

For those of you who like to flip to the back pages of a book to find the ending or the punch line, this is it. Use the text of *The Human Factor* for in-depth descriptions and illustration or flip to the template for possible solutions to your situation.

It has been said there are six phases of the change process:

- Enthusiasm
- Disillusionment
- Growing chaos
- Search for the guilty
- Punishment of the innocent
- Praise for those who did nothing

There must be a better template for reform. Our review of research and best practices has provided time-proven examples of positive change efforts. Even in the midst of reform efforts designed to improve education, some views never change. Comedian Woody Allen has said, "I had a terrible education. I attended a school for emotionally disturbed teachers" (Cohl 1997, 146).

The human factor is that intangible ingredient that separates winners from the losers—or should I say, the successful from the not so successful? We have seen a consistent pattern of change applications exhibited by successful organizations. As leaders, we can only read and study guidelines so much; there comes a time to kick open the door and go to work. Every day that passes without the organization performing to its optimum level is another day where a staff member is left unfulfilled or a child is lost in the system. You can do something about that. There is a definite connection between existing change theory and the efforts of successful organizations. To help sift through what we have examined, here are some highlights of successful change efforts:

- Leadership is necessary to guide change efforts.
- School improvement is about people improvement.
- Some say leaders are born, not made, but research indicates that with an ethical base, positive leadership can be developed.
- Service-centered practices occur when decision making is collaborative.
- Regarding resistance to change: "It is better to light one candle than curse the darkness" (Chinese proverb [Blanchard and Peale 1988, 129]).
- Legislation cannot force excellence.
- Overcome complacency by establishing a sense of urgency.
- A new vision will light the way for a new direction.
- Vision refers to the future, not the past.
- Change takes time.
- If the change will benefit kids, it's worth the fight.
- Student-centered decisions start with a customer-service philosophy.
- Organizational growth occurs when performance shifts from the individual to the team.
- Be hard on problems and soft on people.
- Cheerlead by giving credit to others.
- Sun Tzu wrote that the wise general looks to high ground for battle. He knows invincibility is a matter of defense. So choose your battles wisely and play on your turf (Cleary 1989, 101).
- Resistance is natural. Dissension is healthy when channeled constructively.

- The personal plan for change of my mentor, Don Bagley:
  - First: Get your ducks in line.
  - Second: Trust those you delegate authority to.
  - Third: Don't be afraid to initiate change.
  - Fourth: Trust your instincts.
  - Fifth: Remember change is temporary.
  - Sixth: Don't try to ride a dead horse.

We have investigated how successful schools have changed for the better. We have also found that every school culture is unique. Yet, within every school there are human beings living through the daily struggles of career and family. Such relationships form the basis of the human factor. When used correctly, the human factor can support desired change. We have seen that teachers' attitudes toward change will directly influence the outcomes of the change effort. Understanding that premise, skillful leaders should learn all they can about their teachers in order to develop strategies for implementing change. It is true that change happens. It is also true that carefully planned change implementation strategies are required to bring about desired outcomes. Each school is unique, but the following template serves as a general guide for successful change implementation. This sequential template may be used as a reference to guide the change process from start to finish.

So, leaders, wherever you are—take charge, inspire, hang tough, follow through, and enjoy the change process.

- Accurately assess current conditions to determine:
  - Is change needed?
  - What change is needed?
  - Resistance that may be encountered.
  - Preliminary strategies to overcome resistance.
  - Support from supervisors/parents/community.
  - Identify key leaders in the school.
  - Develop a personal personnel-skills chart to identify all players and their strengths and weaknesses.
- Learn the personal ambitions for each staff member in order to tap into their ambitions and talents.

- Develop a sense of urgency for the areas in need of change. Connect the change effort into the big picture of a service-oriented organization committed to children. Resistance may be minimized either by guilt or commitment when teachers see how children will benefit from the change.
- Create a core group of supporters.
  - Key leaders who believe in the change effort.
  - Gain buy-in by giving respect.
  - Check your ego at the door.
  - Communication builds ownership.
- Share the vision.
- Share specific aspects of the new vision with key leaders.
- Share the big picture with the entire staff.
- Clarify the vision with input from all stakeholders.
- As benchmarks are reached, mission and vision adjust to new directions.
- Create time for necessary planning.
  - Staff.
    - Careful timing of the action plan is essential to reduce the feeling of being overwhelmed.
    - Release time rather than after school.
    - Meet in locations other than school.
  - Committees.
  - Special-interest groups.
  - Time for the leader to keep the change process flowing while attending to the daily tasks of the school.
  - Secure funding that will support teacher planning and training.
  - Don't wait for district-level funding. Remember district funding is like a senior citizen's fixed income. District funding only covers the basics.
- Communicate the vision.
  - It is a continuous process.
  - Use others to spread the word. It's important that many messengers are delivering the same message.
  - One-on-one/group/team/entire staff.
  - Encourage others to try new things.

- Honest communication.
- Develop a school Web page with weekly updates built by your Web design class. Don't have such a class? Make one. The benefits will be far reaching.
- Reorganize staff meetings to become meaningful opportunities for dialogue and problem solving.
- Daily email staff bulletins from the principal. The principal must create a daily communication vehicle whereby the staff has immediate link to the leader.
- Start each message with motivation or humor. Carefully incorporate the vision into announcements and messages.
- Subliminal advertising to keep the vision in the forefront.
- Put data and information in the email bulletins and turn staff meetings into meaningful dialogue covering, if only briefly, each of the following:
  - An instructional strategy from a teacher on staff.
  - A technology application.
  - Caring for students' needs. Discuss any known traumas specific students are undergoing.
  - Caring for staff needs, new babies, illnesses, celebrations.
  - Provide each teacher with a *Professional Educator's Handbook*.
  - For each meeting add a new example of current research, instructional strategies, or motivational techniques and require teachers to bring their handbook to each meeting to update valuable information.
  - Reward staff members. One example may be to secure "dinner for two" prizes and award one at each staff meeting.
  - Build teachers into ambassadors of quality education.
  - Create opportunities to unite the staff around the common cause of customer service.
- Create ownership.
  - Ask for input. Listen for input. Observe interaction.
  - Include entire staff.
  - Build trust by delegating real responsibility, then let go and offer support as needed or requested.
  - Make sure people see you walk the talk.

- Use data to support decisions.
- Secure funds to send teachers to conferences that will benefit the cause and build individual skills.
- Provide a conference feed-back form that teachers must complete upon their return. Provide for a brief teacher synopsis of the conference at staff meetings.
- Focus on small successes to validate the change effort.
- Maintain a feeling of low threat and high service.
- Remain humble and pass recognition to others.
- Timeline.
  - Implement something immediately.
  - Plan an implementation schedule that allows for small changes along the way. This will energize the staff and help them to continue toward the final outcome.
  - Establish a timeline for the major aspects of the change.
  - Share the timeline with the staff so they will become believers as you meet each level of change.
  - Be open to new and better ideas.
  - Communicate constantly.
- Communicate the first changes.
  - Within the school/parents/district/community.
  - Form a partnership with local newspapers and media.
  - Help others to see and believe that initial results validate the entire effort.
- Capitalize on the first success.
  - Continue to build the critical mass of supportive staff.
  - Provide new challenges for staff leaders. Support their interests and share their success.
  - Personally work with and encourage the negative personalities. Show them you may disagree with their ideas but support them as teachers by giving them opportunities to validate their skills.
- Resistance to change.
  - Identify those who oppose and confront them in a factual and positive manner.
  - Personally work with resistors.
  - Give new opportunities and responsibilities to resistors.

- Feed the needs of resistors.
- Counsel out those who cannot get on board.
- Evaluation.
  - Data/testimonial/observation.
  - Share positive experiences with all stakeholders.
  - Use evaluation data to encourage others and to correct problems.
  - Utilize credible staff members to assist with the evaluation.
  - Continuous use of a variety of instruments to determine overall effectiveness of the effort.
- Sustaining the effort.
  - Change is a dynamic phenomenon.
  - Keep building on immediate success.
  - Some changes take time.
  - Hire a staff that matches the new vision.
  - Recognize individual and group successes.
  - Feed the team concept.
  - Reward risk taking.
    - Build in 10 percent administrative costs for teachers who write successful grants.
    - Restaurant gift certificates.
    - Present individual awards at staff meetings.
  - Maximize the new staff enthusiasm.
  - Be creative and design something for everyone.
  - Build leadership capacity in as many people as possible.
  - Be persistent/hold the course.
  - Be committed to the fact that the effort is worth fighting for.

Finally, change, vision, and leadership go hand in hand. Whether turning around a troubled school, changing a specific segment within the school, or building a new school, personal commitment is essential. Change does require leadership.

Throughout *The Human Factor in Change*, we have found personal interaction to be a crucial element of the change process. We have also seen that strong leadership is required to guide significant change efforts. When leaders understand the dynamics of human interaction, environments can be created in which people work together believing in a common cause. It is inevitable that change will happen. The challenge for leaders is to direct change efforts to produce desirable outcomes. Implementing change can be the most difficult challenge of your career. Even in the best situation, change is difficult. The stakes are high, for as long as a single child lacks the opportunity to become the best he or she can be, conditions must be improved— and change is not an option but a requirement.

REFERENCES

Adams, Robert M. (1992). *The Prince by Niccolo Machiavelli* (2nd ed.). New York: W. W. Norton.

Bangert-Downs, Robert L., and Lawrence M. Rudner. (1991). *Meta-Analysis in Educational Research.* ERIC Clearinghouse on Assessment and Evaluation. http://ericae.net.

Bartlett's Familiar Quotations. (2002). *Joseph Addison.* Cato. Act. II. Sc. 4. Yahoo References.

Bellott, F. K., and F. D. Tutor. (1990). "A Challenge to the Conventional Wisdom of Herzburg and Maslow Theories." Paper presented at the Nineteenth Annual Meeting of the Mid-South Educational Research Association, New Orleans, Louisiana.

Bennett, William J. (1999). *Our Country's Founders.* New York: Scholastic.

Bennis, Warren, and Burt Nanus. (1985). *Leaders: The Strategies for Taking Charge.* New York: Harper & Row.

Blanchard, Kenneth, and Don Shula. (1995). *Everyone's a Coach.* Grand Rapids, Mich.: Zondervan.

Blanchard, Kenneth, and Norman Vincent Peale. (1988). *The Power of Ethical Management.* New York: William Morrow.

Bodilly, S., B. Keltner, Reichardt Purnell, and G. Schuyler. (1998). Reforming America's Schools. Observations on Implementing "Whole School Designs." Santa Monica, Calif.: RAND. *Lessons from New American School's Scale-up Phase: Prospects for Bringing Designs to Multiple Schools.* Research brief done within RAND Education.

Bolman, Lee G., and Terrance E. Deal. (1995). *Leading with Soul.* San Francisco: Jossey-Bass.

Boyer, Ernest. (1985). "In the Aftermath of Excellence," *Educational Leadership*. In R. DuFour and R. Eaker, *Creating the New American School: A Principal's Guide to School Improvement* (pp. 10–13). Bloomington, Ind.: National Education Service.

Brownlow, Paul C., ed. (1997). *Strength for a Man's Heart*. Fort Worth, Tex.: Brownlow.

Burns, James McGregor. (1978). *Leadership*. New York: Harper & Row.

California Department of Education, Office of School Recognition Program. (1999). *Distinguished Schools*. Sacramento: California Department of Education.

Chubb, J., and Moe, T. (1991). *Politics, Markets, and America's Schools*. In M. Mathews and P. J. Karr-Kidwell, *The New Technology and Education Reform: Guidelines for School Administrators*. Washington, D.C.: Office of Educational Research and Improvement.

Claremont Institute. Statesman Archive. (2001). *Speech before the Republican State Convention: The House Divided*. www.claremont.org.

Cleary, Thomas. (1989). *Mastering the Art of War*. Boston: Shambhala.

Cohl, Aaron H. (1997). *The Friars Club Encyclopedia of Jokes*. New York: Black Dog and Leventhal.

Coutu, Diane. (2001). The Anxiety of Learning. *Harvard Business Review*, 5. March 1, 2002.

Covey, Stephen R. (1990a). *The 7 Habits of Highly Effective People*. New York: Fireside Simon and Schuster.

Covey, Stephen R. (1990b). *Principle-Centered Leadership*. New York: Fireside Simon and Schuster.

Croteau, Maureen, and Wayne Worcester. (1993). *The Essential Researcher*. New York: Harper Perennial.

Crouch, Van. (1995). *Winning 101*. Tulsa, Okla.: Honor Books.

Delsohn, Steve. (2001). *True Blue*. New York: HarperCollins.

Dimun, Bonnie. (1998). *Educational Marketing: An Essential Tool for Managing Change*. Princeton, N.J.: Princeton University, Press.

DuFour, Richard, and Robert Eaker. (1992). *Creating the New American School: A Principal's Guide to School Improvement*. Bloomington, Ind.: National Educational Service.

Freed, Jann E. (1997). "Legends in Their Own Minds." *Training*, 16.

Freed, Jann E. (1998). *The Challenge of Change: Creating a Quality Culture*. Washington, D.C.: U.S. Department of Education, Office of Educational Research and Improvement.

Fulghum, Robert. (1997). *Words I Wish I Wrote*. New York: HarperCollins.

Gawel, Joseph E. (1997). *Herzberg's Theory of Motivation and Maslow's Hierarchy of Needs.* Practical Assessment, Research and Evaluation. ERIC Clearinghouse on Assessment and Evaluation.

Goodman, Edward C., ed. (1997). *The Forbes Book of Business Quotations: 14, 266 Thoughts on the Business of Life.* New York: Black Day & Leventhal Publishers.

Hagberg Consulting Group. (2001). *Best Leaders.* www.hegnet.com.

Hill, Paul T. (1995). *Reinventing Public Education.* Policy brief by RAND Institute on Education and Training. www.rand.org

Ho Kwok Man, Joanne O'Brien, and Martin Palmer. (1986). *The Fortune Teller's I Ching.* London: Random House.

Holtz, Lou. (1998). *Winning Every Day.* New York: HarperCollins.

Jones, Laurie Beth. (1995). *Jesus CEO: Using Ancient Wisdom for Visionary Leadership.* New York: Hyperion.

Karr-Kidwell, P. J., and Mark Matthews. (1999). *The New Technology and Educational Reform: Guidelines for School Administrators.* Washington, D.C.: Office of Educational Research and Improvement.

Katzenbach, Jon R., and Douglas K. Smith. (1993). *The Wisdom of Teams.* New York: HarperCollins.

Kim, Daniel, ed. (1999). *The System Thinker.* In A. Kleiner, C. Roberts, R. B. Ross, P. M. Senge, and B. J. Smith, *The Fifth Discipline.* New York: Currency Doubleday.

Kleiner, Art, Charlotte Roberts, Richard B. Ross, Peter M. Senge, and Bryan J. Smith. (1994). *The Fifth Discipline.* New York: Currency Doubleday.

Kotter, John P. (1996). *Leading Change.* Boston: Harvard Business School Press.

Krzyzewski, Mike. (2000). *Leading with the Heart.* New York: Warner Books.

Leonard, R., H. Shulman, and G. Smith. (1996). *Application of F-117 Acquisition Strategy to Other Programs in the New Acquisition Environment.* Research brief for RAND's Project AIR FORCE.

Lombardi, Vince. http://vincelombardi.com.

Martin Luther King Jr. *20th Century U.S. History.* http://members.aol.com/klove01/martinsp.htm.

Matthews, M., and P. J. Karr-Kidwell. (1999). *The New Technology and Education Reform: Guidelines for School Administrators.* Washington, D.C.: Office of Educational Research and Improvement.

McAdams, R. P. (1997). A Systems Approach to School Reform. *Phi Delta Kappan,* 79(2): 28–33.

McLaughlin, Milbrey. (1990). The Rand Change Agent Study Revisited: Macro Perspectives and Micro Realities. In R. Dufour and R. Eaker, *Creating the New*

American School: A Principal's Guide to School Improvement (p. 20). Bloomington, Ind.: National Education Service.

MotivationalQuotes.com. (2003). Mark Twain. *Imagination.* Accessed March 12,
2003.

MSNBC, Newsweek, March 18, 2002.

National Archives and Records Administration. Abraham Lincoln. www.archives.gov.
Accessed August 2003.

National Archives and Records Administration. The Constitution: Amendments
14. www.archives.gov. Accessed August 2003.

National Archives and Records Administration. Dred Scott. www.archives.gov. Accessed August 2003.

National Archives and Records Administration. John F. Kennedy. www.archives.gov.
Accessed August 2003.

National Archives and Records Administration. Robert Kennedy. www.archives.gov.
Accessed August 2003.

National Archives and Records Administration. Women's Suffrage and the 19th
Amendment. www.archives.gov. Accessed August 2003.

NIV Topical Study Bible. (1989). Grand Rapids, Mich.: Zondervan.

Peal, Norman Vincent. (1986). *Why Some Positive Thinkers Get Powerful Results.*
Nashville, Tenn.: Oliver-Nelson Books.

Peters, Tom. (1987). *Thriving on Chaos: Handbook for a Management Revolution.*
New York: HarperCollins.

Platt, Suzy. (1993). *Respectfully Quoted.* New York: Barnes and Noble.

Prahalad, C. K., and Allan Hammond. (2002). Serving the World's Poor, Profitably.
Harvard Business Review, September 2.

Respectfully Quoted. (1993). Barnes and Noble.

Rhodes, Lewis A. (1990). Beyond Your Beliefs: Quantum Leaps toward Quality
Schools. *School Administrator*, December 26.

Schein, Edgar H. (1965). *Organizational Psychology.* Upper Saddle River, N.J.:
Prentice Hall.

Schlechty, Phillip. (1990). *Schools for the 21st Century: Leadership Imperatives for
Educational Reform.* In R. Dufour and R. Eaker, *Creating the New American
School: A Principal's Guide to School Improvement* (p. 10). Bloomington, Ind.:
National Education Service.

Schmoker, Mike. (1996). *Results: The Key to Continuous School Improvement.*
Alexandria, Va.: Association for Supervision and Curriculum Development.

School Services of California. (1998). *Fiscal Aspects of Negotiations.* Sacramento:
School Services of California.

Seferian, Robert. (1999). *Design and Implementation of a Social-Skills Program for Middle School Students with Learning and Behavioral Disabilities.* Fort Lauderdale, Fl.: Nova Southeastern University.

Short, Bo. (1997). *The Foundation of Leadership.* Alexandria, Va.: Excalibur.

Thorndike-Barnhart Dictionary Series. (1984). *World Book Dictionary.* Chicago: Doubleday.

Traub, James. (1999). *Better by Design? A Consumer's Guide to Schoolwide Reform.* Washington, D.C.: Thomas B. Fordham Foundation.

Ulich, Robert. (1954). *Three Thousand Years of Educational Wisdom* (2nd ed.). Cambridge, Mass.: Harvard University Press.

U.S. Census Bureau. (2001). *Population Division.* www.census.gov. Accessed August 2003.

U.S. State Department. (2002). Thinkquest.org. Accessed August 2003.

Weick, K. E. (1982). Administering Education in Loosely Coupled Schools. *Phi Delta Kappan, 66*(4): 673–76.

Wooden, John. (1972). *They Call Me Coach.* Waco, Tex.: Word.

Yee, Jennifer Agnes. (1998). *Forcers Motivating Institutional Reform.* ERIC Digest.

Zimbalist, Ronald. (2001). *The Dynamics of Organizational Change: A Study of How California Distinguished Schools Use Change to Implement Positive New Outcomes.* Santa Barbara, Calif.: University of Santa Barbara.

INDEX

ABOUT THE AUTHOR

The pursuit of change is actually a personal journey toward an improved condition. *The Human Factor in Change* describes how skillful leaders use the change process to build relationships within their organizations that eventually lead to systemic reform. Through a career spanning thirty years in education, Dr. Ron Zimbalist has been a change agent building a vision for schools that includes innovation and opportunities for all children. Selected as regional administrator of the year, distinguished principal, and three years as principal of the year, Zimbalist has brought his vision and leadership to public education by designing and opening new schools, while guiding teachers to develop award-winning learning communities.

A speaker at state and national conferences, Zimbalist has demonstrated models of innovation from technology to academic interventions. From his experiences as a business owner and educator, he illustrates how desirable change requires leadership—yet leadership is not for everyone. So why take on the burden and responsibilities of leadership? The answer is simple. You'll never really understand until you've been there. When you believe and see how leadership is actually a privilege that can improve lives, then you will understand the essence of the human factor in change.